Indian pueblos

Spanish towns and villages

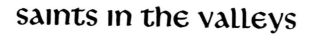

saints in the valleys

Cristo Crucificado. Height: 23¼″. Mora Group, Author's Collection.

saints in the

valleys
christian sacred images

in the history, life and folk art

of spanish new mexico

JOSE E. ESPINOSA

the university of new mexico press - 1960

THE PUBLICATION OF THIS BOOK IS MADE POSSIBLE BY A GRANT FROM THE FORD FOUNDATION

composed, printed and bound at the university of new mexico printing plant, albuquerque, new mexico, u.s.a.

library of congress catalog card number 60-5656, first edition.

A LA MEMORIA DE MIS PADRES

Celso Espinosa y Montoya

Rafaela Martínez Valdez

NUEVOMEXICANOS Y DEVOTOS DE LOS SANTOS

contents

ILLUSTRATIONS

fOREWORÒ

THE HOMEMADE PERSONABLE SAINTS of New Mexico, sage symbols of thought-and-life patterns a century and a half ago, have so taken hold of people's interest in our time as to become collectors' items on the one hand and the nucleus of a small science on the other. I regard them as homemade because one cannot imagine their having been produced in special workshops, even little ones, but fashioned in cozy kitchens during the winter months and, in summer weather, underneath spreading cottonwoods by adobe walls splashed with sun. To me their being personable is not from any comeliness, which so many of them lack, but from their having been born out of a deep-felt spiritual need, in their creators as well as in the persons requesting them, and not from any purely commercial motive or even for art's sake alone. In this idea of hearth and heart, I am sure, lies the secret of their appeal, and of their worth.

Hence, any attempt to reproduce these *santos* now, even by native New Mexicans, or to revive similar carvings as an "art," is not only a sin against art itself, but a mockery in its best results.

Their having been sought out by collectors, for several decades already, has proved to be a mixed blessing. In an "autobiography" of *La Conquistadora,* that beloved and famous ancient image of the Virgin in Santa Fe, I had her quail with alarm at being classed with these homemade *santos,* the collecting of which had "become a fad, almost like that of collecting old shaving mugs," while the very word *santo* had become "an arty byword for sacred images." This was her protest, and mine, at a kind of practice which began laudably with discerning persons, people who collected them for their spiritual as well as artistic value, but which ended with the collecting for collecting's sake among shallow-souled imitators of the real collector, with the intermediate traffic of filching, horsetrading, faking, and all else that is shady and banal in rackets. However, one has to admit that, were it not for the collector, even the despicable sort, a great many of these saints would have vanished forever.

Private collections tend to come together and form major bodies when their owners finally will them to museums, and these bodies continue growing with the addition of individual pieces by further donation, purchase, or as the fruit of deliberate exploration and discovery. The NewMexico saints were no exception to this fate. Now began a phase of classification and interpretation. Occasional articles or chapters on the subject written before were succeeded by more pretentious and specialized monographs and books. While all of these writings have approached the subject with due respect for the *santos'* religious meaning, and often a strange secular affection for their little wooden selves, too many of them attain a ridiculous eminence because their respective authors lacked a genuine grasp of the idea behind the Catholic veneration (not worship) of the saints, not to mention the depth and scope of scholarly background and research needed for such a task. A prime example of this is a recent monograph, beautifully printed, which was put out by a large museum (outside New Mexico). It starts out with this kind of historical statement in the preface: ". . . the churches of the area were taken from the Mexican colonial diocese and placed under Catholic bishops." Perhaps the printer dropped the word "American" that should have preceded "Catholic bishops." But the very first subject and illustration is not a printer's mistake. Here a carved stick with three woodpeckers, not a religious symbol by any means, is pompously palmed off as the Holy Trinity! I am sure if the number had been a dozen woodpeckers, the identification would have been given as the Twelve Apostles.

Fortunately, there are some *aficionados* of the *santos* who approach their subject with a scholarly caution equal to their fine enthusiasm, like Wilder, Stallings, and Boyd. They bring to bear on their dating and classifying all the tools of documentary and archaeological research at their command. Their few mistakes are honest ones, common to all human endeavor, and ready to be righted with the advent of new evidence. Their reverence is remarkable, a rare gift of sympathy, since they do not share the same beliefs with the *santeros*. Theirs is that small science mentioned at the start of this commentary. Their writings, as a result, are not pocked by woodpeckers.

Still, all their knowledge and skill, their great devotion, cannot engender a further qualification needed to crown their great work. By becoming Catholics they might come closer to it. But they cannot be reborn fifty years back on the same soil and atmosphere that nurtured the blood of the *santero* as well as the tree from which the *santo* came. Fortunately, again, we have such a person in Dr. Espinosa who, having acquired the tools and qualifications of a scholar after many years of study and teaching in major universities outside his native state, never forgot the loving inner kindred ties he has with the saints in the valleys and hills of home. While he may not, at that great distance, surpass the few experts in dating or identifying this or that particular piece, his mind and heart penetrate every dried cell inside those personable, if homely, little faces and figures. To him, and to me, they are not queer fetishes for an ethnological alcove in a museum, nor yet objects of art to lend atmosphere to a southwestern fireplace. They are dear relics of a Faith and a People in a certain time and place, a dimension to which our blood and faith can transfer us at will, and as legitimate and touching as those first attempts to portray the Saviour and His saints on the walls of the catacombs.

Fray Angélico Chávez, O.F.M.

preface

DURING THE PAST TWENTY-FIVE YEARS the religious folk art of Spanish New Mexico, the execution of which spanned a period of some one hundred twenty-five years from about 1775 to 1900, has advanced beyond the attentions of local curators, curio dealers and amateur antiquarians, to attract the interest of art critics, historians of art, learned journals, popular magazines, and some of our more important art museums.

The compelling narrative of this art, which is the only religious art indigenous to the present-day United States, has not been heretofore either investigated or presented in a manner approaching its full scope. This volume is an effort to trace the history of sacred images in Spanish-Colonial New Mexico, and thus to furnish the background necessary to present properly the role of the saints in the life and folk art of the Spanish and Mexican colonials who, from 1598 on, settled in the area to-day embraced by the borders of New Mexico and in the San Luis Valley of southern Colorado.

The art of the New Mexican folk image-maker falls into two principal aesthetic categories: The first includes those paintings and statues which are of simple and often crude aspect. These archaic-looking works may be compared to Christian art from the days of the catacombs to about the year 1200, especially that of the frescoes, manuscripts, and wooden statuary. A second category is made up of those flat paintings and statues which tend toward greater realism, and which display both talent and skill. The panels of this category are often as delicate and lovely as the figures on old porcelain, and the statues take on the life and drama of Spanish baroque statuary.

The motivation of the New Mexican folk artist is analogous to that of the carvers and painters of medieval Europe in that he did not establish as his goal, and therefore did not always achieve, convincing likenesses. His principal motive, like that of the artists of early Christian times, was to convey the messages of Christianity. New Mexican religious folk art, as does all folk art, tends toward simplicity of statement, and toward unadorned, often stark representation of the feelings of the artist. Photographic realism is not always attained, the result often being an abstract and stylistic art. In flat paintings there is little illusion of depth, figures are drawn with scant attention to space, and the face of nearly every figure is in full view. New Mexican statuary has almost its exact counterpart in the polychromed wooden figures of Europe of the twelfth, thirteenth, and fourteenth centuries, examples of which may be seen in any large museum collection. Throughout Spanish America also, from Argentina to Mexico and in the Caribbean area, innumerable examples may be found of folk statuary which closely resemble the archaic-looking figures in the round of New Mexico. It cannot be stated too often that there is little originality in New Mexican *santos,* for their every reflection, technical and artistic, issues from some facet of European or Mexican religious art.

The adjective "primitive" should not be used to describe New Mexican *santos,* for these images form a procession of ever-changing styles and concepts far removed from the similar habits of visualization which characterize the work of primitive artisans.

New Mexican *santos* appeal to the intellect just as much as they plead with the emotions, for *santeros,* to the same extent as artists of the schools, expressed in their work their beliefs and ideas. The *santeros* did not paint and carve for relaxation or amusement, but to externalize for themselves and their people deeply-felt spiritual convictions, which, though beyond their own explanation, issued from an extensively practiced, studied and documented complex of philosophical and theological principles.

New Mexican *santos,* like all Christian images, were intended to function as vincula between God and His creatures by evoking the personalities of Christ, His mother and the saints, coming into existence without artistic theory and unaccompanied by the ends of profane art. When isolation and relative poverty deprived them of any other means of securing sacred images, the accumulated momentum of almost seventeen centuries of Christian experience impelled the New Mexicans to make their own simple but meaningful representations. Their folk art was not imposed upon their religious practices, but on the contrary issued from those practices. If New Mexican *santos* are unfit to represent Christ, the Virgin and the saints, as is sometimes heard, then neither are many of the drawings and frescoes on the walls of the Roman catacombs, nor many European sacred representations executed before the Renaissance, including some of the most ancient and venerated.

New Mexican religious folk art was periodic and local, within the framework of a faith which is timeless and universal. Historically and religiously, the importance of this art lies in its being such a sincere and complete expression of the spirit which produced it. The old *santos* of New Mexico were made during a certain time, and their form reflects the social, economic, political and religious forces of that time. Their beauty emanates from within the spirit in which they were fashioned, and this attraction, once understood, invests the old *santos* of New Mexico with a spiritual grace and elegance which is unmistakably present to those who share, even in part, the faith of the folk who made them.

xiii

ACKNOWLEDGMENTS. Many statements of gratitude and recognition are scattered throughout the text and footnotes, yet it would be little short of dishonest not to mention those individuals who have made special contributions to this volume: E. Boyd, Curator, Department of Spanish Colonial Arts, Museum of New Mexico, for constant and invaluable assistance. Mrs. Helen Chandler Ryan, formerly Director, Harwood Foundation, Taos, for so much help during my visits to northern New Mexico. Miss Carmen Gertrudis Espinosa, Albuquerque, for turning over to me the voluminous notes and transcriptions taken and made by her over a period of years from old records in the Land Office in Santa Fe. Gilbert Espinosa, Albuquerque, for placing at my disposal his precious collection of *santos* which served as the original inspiration of this study. Robert Clogg, Detroit, Michigan, without whose advice the photographic work related to this volume scarcely would have been possible. To the editorial staff of the University of New Mexico Press, especially Ramona Maher Martinez, whose skills and interest have been a continuing source of support and encouragement. Lastly, my *paisanos* in the hills, mountains, valleys and plains of northern New Mexico and southern Colorado who were ever ready to give me of their time and energy, which went so far to make my work in their homes and chapels so pleasant and rewarding.

JOSÉ E. ESPINOSA

University of Detroit

saints in the valleys

Dichoso árbol verdadero
dichoso árbol de la luz,
dichoso árbol prodigioso,
donde murió mi Jesús.

Oh blessed Tree of Truth,
oh Tree of Light to guide,
oh blessed Tree Prodigious,
where my Jesus died.

　　　　—New Mexican folk hymn.

2

ABBReVIATIONS

ABBREVIATIONS USED FOR WORKS FREQUENTLY CITED FOR ILLUSTRATIONS

ABC: E. Boyd, *Retablos. The Alfred I. Barton Collection,* Miami Beach, Fla. [1951].

APR: Willard Hougland, *Santos. A Primitive American Art* [New York, 1946].

EP: *El Palacio,* published by the School of American Research, Santa Fe.

MMNM: Edgar L. Hewett and Reginald G. Fisher, *Mission Monuments of New Mexico,* Albuquerque, 1943.

RFA: Mitchell A. Wilder with Edgar Breitenbach, *Santos, The Religious Folk Art of New Mexico,* Colorado Springs, 1943.

SOS: *Santos of the Southwest,* The Denver Art Museum, Denver, 1953.

SSM: E. Boyd, *Saints and Saint Makers of New Mexico,* Laboratory of Anthropology Santa Fe, 1946.

historical introduction

THE EARLY HISTORY OF SACRED IMAGES IN NEW MEXICO

THE DEARTH of relevant documentary materials renders trackless the exploration of the story of sacred images in New Mexico for the first eighty-five years of her history dating from the entry of Coronado in 1540. No images are mentioned in the narratives of the first six expeditions into that territory from Fray Marcos de Niza in 1539 through the entries of Bonilla and Gutiérrez de Humaña in 1593, although the practice of carrying images unquestionably prevailed on these journeys of discovery and investigation.

The first mention of sacred images in New Mexican history is found in Villagrá's epic of the Oñate expedition of 1598 which resulted in the founding of the New Mexican colony, a mere reference to two simulacra.[1]

The earliest list of paintings and statuary is part of the record of supplies for the Franciscan missionaries going to New Mexico under Fray Alonso de Benavides in 1624, twenty-five years after the founding of the colony. Sporadic reference to images is made between this Franciscan record and the Pueblo Revolt of 1680, some of this material offering valuable information up to that date. The late seventeenth century gives us detailed accounts of the many images destroyed or mutilated during the Pueblo uprising, and of those recovered incident to the retreat and attempted reconquest under Otermín in 1681 and the reconquest under Vargas in 1692, 1693, and 1696. Other records of the same century, both civil and ecclesiastical, refer to church furnishing of every description.

Of the many official reports, narratives and communications of the eighteenth century, only one, the Domínguez report of 1776, contains information relating to sacred images. This recently published document is an outstanding contribution to the history of New Mexico during the eighteenth century, and is replete with materials related to our subject, and is, therefore, fully exploited in a number of fundamental respects.

Some one hundred and fifty wills filed between 1704 and 1843 provide for the disposition of sacred images of every sort, and together with the church inventories of April 21-August 27, 1796, and June 5-July 28, 1808, are of real value.

Paintings on animal skins are included in several wills. These images were first executed during the days of the establishment of the colony (1598–1610). Considering that there were 112 paintings on animal skins listed in the Domínguez report alone, painted skins must have been commonly done during the years following the reconquest of 1692 also, a plain indication of the constant need for sacred representations from the time of the first settlements.

---

1. In the lists of supplies drawn up during the several inspections of the Oñate army in 1596 and 1597 there appear hundreds of rosaries, agnus deis and medals under the headings "Articles for trading" and "Articles for barter." These are not sacred images in the meaning required by this study.

THE ADVENT
OF NEW MEXICAN
RELIGIOUS FOLK ART

Sometime during the third quarter of the eighteenth century there appeared in what is today New Mexico a religious folk art in the form of images carved in the round of pine and cottonwood, coated with *yeso* (gesso), and painted with water-solvent colors (tempera), bas-reliefs of modeled *yeso* on pine panels painted with tempera colors, and paintings in the same medium on *yeso*-coated pine panels. An image in the round is called a *bulto*. A modeled bas-relief or a flat painting on a pine panel is called a *retablo*. A group of painted panels or of images in the round, or a combination of these, used for what is known in English as an altar-screen, retable, or reredos, is also called a *retablo*.

In Spanish the generic name for any sacred image is *santo*. The word has several meanings throughout the Spanish-speaking world, but there is nothing colloquial about its use in New Mexico to identify sacred images in any form, as some writers on *santos* imply.

The derivative *santero* also has a number of meanings in the Hispanic world, the primary one being the caretaker of a sanctuary, and, therefore, a person whose duties would involve the care of sacred images. In several areas of Spanish America the name is also applied to one who makes or repairs sacred images.[2] This is the meaning of the word in New Mexico, but it is never applied to an artist of academic training. The word *santería* as used in the present writing is intended to mean the place where sacred images are made, or the art of making them.

The makers of New Mexican *santos* were the frequently poor, unlettered farmers, villagers and peasants of the Upper Rio Grande Valley, of the Mora Valley to the east across the Sangre de Cristo Range, and of the Tomé area in the Lower Rio Grande Valley. A late type of *bulto* with glass eyes appeared in southern Colorado toward the end of the nineteenth century. Any village in these areas could have been the home of a *santero*. The fact that no supply of sacred images was available to satisfy the demands of the devout inhabitants of the isolated and craftless province is the simple and obvious circumstance which accounts for their advent.

It has been stated and restated by writers of articles in popular magazines that New Mexican *santos* are the product of Indian craftsmanship. The New Mexican Indian, quite at variance with the proclivities of the Mexican Indian, was never attracted to the making of Christian images. In the few instances where Christian symbols are found in Indian art, such as in the Cueva Pintada near El Rito de los Frijoles and in some of the pueblo churches, it is clear from their disposition that the decorative element was the point of attraction, and certainly not the abstractions of Christian symbolism. This absence of New Mexican Indian interest in the making of Christian sacred images is merely another reflection of his unwillingness to accept Christian religious practices in general, an attitude which he has consistently maintained since his earliest contacts with the Franciscan missionaries.[3]

The golden age of *santo*-making was from about 1795 to about 1860, after which time the art declined in both quality and quantity, fading out completely in the last decade of the nineteenth century.

SANTOS
AND EARLY VISITORS
TO NEW MEXICO FROM
THE UNITED STATES

The few strangers who wandered into New Mexico during the waning years of the

2. "Persona que tiene por oficio fabricar santos de madera, o retocarlos, etc.," Santamaría, *Diccionario General de Americanismos,* Méjico, 1942.

3. ". . . the Christianization of the Indians was hardly more than a superficial conformity to a few outward practices which they did not understand or have much interest in." Eleanor B. Adams, "Bishop Tamaron's Visitation to New Mexico, 1760," *New Mexico Historical Review,* XXVIII, 2 (April, 1953), 111.

eighteenth century left no record of their ex-
periences, so we do not know whether any of
them took notice of the religious folk art
there which was then well past its genesis.
Even in the detailed accounts of Pike, written
in the opening decade of the nineteenth century, there is no mention of *santos*. On the
heels of Pike, a large number of English-
speaking Americans and French Canadians
settled in New Mexico. Many of them lived
in intimate contact with the New Mexican
people, but of the few who left a written account of any kind, none took the least notice
of the religious folk art which surrounded
him. From 1822 on, the Santa Fe Trail
brought into New Mexico scores of men from
the States who made comfortable livings, if
not modest fortunes, engaging in the lucrative
trade of those colorful days. A number of
these traders, notably Josiah Gregg and
James Josiah Webb, left descriptive records
of their journeys and observations, but, again,
not one of them mentioned *santos* in his
writings.

The last fifty-five years of the nineteenth
century saw the writing and publication of a
rather extensive list of reports and personal
narratives by historians, invading soldiers,
explorers, adventurers, and travelers on every
phase of New Mexican life. Most of these
men (and one woman) had occasion to observe the interiors of the homes, the chapels,
and the churches, and several of them, particularly W. H. Emory (1846), W. W.
H. Davis (1853–57), James F. Meline
(1866), John Gregory Bourke (1881), and
L. Bradford Prince (1888), make very
pointed references to New Mexican religious
folk art; Emory, Davis, and Bourke, among
others, in the most uncomplimentary terms.
Meline is almost unique among these ob-
servers in that he viewed the handiwork of
the *santero* with sympathy and understanding.

Without documentary foundation, writers
keep repeating that when Father Jean Bap-
tiste Lamy came to Santa Fe as vicar in 1851
his reaction to New Mexican religious statuary and paintings was so negative that he
ordered them removed from the chapels and
churches of the territory. The fact that the
rural chapels of both the Upper and Lower
Rio Grande valleys have never been without
folk-made images since their appearance
argues against accepting the statement that a
blanket order to remove them was issued.

THE COLLECTING
OF SANTOS

The first collector of New Mexican religious folk art of whom we have any knowledge, and apparently a lone figure in the field
for some thirty years, was one Samuel Eldodt,
a trader who began as storekeeper at San Juan
Pueblo around 1868. This fact is mentioned
by Bourke in his journal for July, 1881, at
which time Eldodt had been at San Juan for
thirteen years. Some of the images of the
Norma Fiske Day Collection, now in the
Museum of New Mexico, are said to have
belonged to Eldodt. Bourke himself may have
collected *santos*, for we know that he bought
a painted skin on one occasion.

The turn of the present century welcomed
the arrival of general interest in the collection
and preservation of *santos* by individual en-
thusiasts, amateur antiquarians, dealers in
New Mexican curios, organizations, and institutions, pioneered, it seems, by the New
Mexico Historical Society. During the past
twenty-five years interest in *santos* has been
aroused from coast to coast, and exhibitions
have been held in almost every principal city
of the nation.

TWENTIETH-CENTURY
LITERATURE ON SANTOS

The present century has produced a vast
catalogue of literature relating to every aspect of New Mexican history. Up to the present writing some eighty-two studies have been
devoted to New Mexican religious folk art.
The authors of these publications, which are
mainly short, often one- to two-page monographs, are the pioneer workers on the slowly

but surely rising structure of *santo* literature. The most significant studies to date are the articles, monographs, booklets and one volume of E. Boyd, twenty-two in all, the booklet by Wilder, and one volume by Wilder with Breitenbach, all listed in the Bibliography. Only a small part of the remaining literature contains materials of much value, being so filled with misinformation, invention, and repetition of errors that it would not be proper to recommend it.[4]

---

4. As recently as 1949 (*New Mexico Historical Review*, XXIV, 3, for July) there appeared an article titled "New Mexico in Transition." Pages 209-11 repeat the same old misconceptions: *Santeros* were taught by the friars; identifies old skin paintings as the work of *santeros*; states that from 1700 to 1835 the work of at least thirty professional *santeros* can be identified; that by the middle of the nineteenth century *santeros* had ceased to be, etc.

1. settlement & prelude to disaster
1539-1680

THE SPANISH DISCOVERERS, conquerors and colonizers of the New World, and the missionaries who accompanied them, possessed a complete understanding of the place of sacred images in the liturgical and devotional practices of their Catholic faith, and took with them to the most distant outposts of empire representations of Christ, the Virgin and the saints.

When Cortez landed on the coast of Mexico in 1519, he and his men carried with them a variety of Christian sacred images. Díaz del Castillo, one of Cortez' captains, relates that shortly after the battle of Cintla (March 25, 1519) the *conquistador* told the Indians "how we were Christians and worshiped one true and only God, and he showed them a much revered image of Our Lady with her precious Son in her arms and explained to them that we paid the greatest reverence to that holy image because it represented the Mother of Our Lord God who is in heaven."[1] This image was set up on specially constructed altars all along the line of march to the capital of Montezuma. Cortez showed it to the Aztec emperor, and kept it in his own quarters in the Mexican capital. Later on, this same image was set up in the principal Aztec temple. While Cortez was away from the capital the Aztecs revolted, and upon his return one of the assaults was against this same temple, where the Mexicans had stationed themselves to protect their idols. "Our Lord willed," says Díaz del Castillo, "that we reached the place where we used to keep the image of Our Lady,

and we did not find it; and it appears, as we came to know, that the great Montezuma either was devoted to it or was afraid of it, and ordered the image kept in a safe place."[2]

With the fall of the Aztec capital on August 13, 1521, the Spaniards set about to reconstruct the city, seven-eighths of which the three months' siege had reduced to ruins. In less than four years a new city had risen, and although not as large as the former capital, it surpassed it in beauty and strength. By 1525 Mexico City had taken on the characteristics of a Spanish municipality. On the site of the temple of the Aztec war god was built the first Christian church in Mexico, San Francisco el Grande, and the first cathedral was dedicated in honor of the Immaculate Conception by the first Archbishop of Mexico, Fray Juan de Zumárraga, about 1530. The speed with which these works were undertaken and completed gives evidence of the presence of many skilled artisans among those who came with Cortez and of those who later joined his army before the final assault on the city. Within a few years a number of craftsmen, artists and scientists from Spain and other nations of Europe collaborated in the task of erecting and adorning the churches, cathedrals, public buildings and homes of New Spain. The natives did a sizeable portion of the work, as their own architectual skills and craftsmanship in general was of a high order before the Spaniards arrived. By the close of

1. *Verdadera Historia*, Chap. XXXVI.
2. *Ibid.*, Chap. CXXVI.

the sixteenth century the Mexicans had also developed great skills in all of the Spanish arts and crafts, such as wood carving, ironworking and painting.

The Spanish *conquistadores*, ever alert to any opportunities for new Mexicos to conquer, listened to the exaggerated tales of Alvar Núñez Cabeza de Vaca, who, eight years out of Florida as one of the four survivors of the ill-fated Narváez expedition, wandered into Culiacán, Mexico, with yarns of fabled regions to the north. Cabeza de Vaca had not visited New Mexico, but he was the first European to approach the region about which much had been heard some years before.

Antonio de Mendoza, the viceroy of Mexico, immediately set afoot plans for northern exploration, but these did not materialize until 1539 when he instructed Francisco Vázquez de Coronado, then governor of Nueva Galicia, to effect preliminary investigations. Fray Marcos de Niza, a Franciscan who had accompanied Pizarro to Peru, set out from San Miguel de Culiacán on March 7 of the same year. With him went the Negro, Estevanico, who had accompanied Cabeza de Vaca on the long trek back from the Narváez disaster, and a number of Indians. Estevanico preceded the friar as scout, and according to plan sent back a large cross as a sign that he had found the Seven Cities of Cíbola previously reported by Vaca. Fray Marcos quickened his steps, viewing from a near-by hill the sun-parched pueblo of Zuñi, and learned that his guide had been killed by the natives. Returning to Mexico he reported to the viceroy on September 2 that the Seven Cities were richer than Mexico City itself.

Any number of adventurers immediately petitioned for the right to explore the region. Among the aspirants were Cortez, Gonzalo Nuño de Guzmán, Pedro de Alvarado, one of Cortez' best officers, and Hernando de Soto, who was to discover the Mississippi one year before his death in 1542. Charles V, however, decided to have the exploring done in the name of the crown, and commissioned Coronado to head the expedition.

In February, 1540, Coronado set out from Compostela with two hundred horsemen, seventy foot soldiers, and nine hundred Indians. He reached Cíbola early in July, but instead of great cities rich with emeralds and gold he found only the poverty-stricken village of Hawikuh, about fifteen miles southwest of Zuñi. He left for the interior while Hernando de Alarcón, one of his lieutenants, ascended the Colorado River for about two hundred miles, and another officer, Melchor Díaz, explored as far as Yuma in present-day Arizona. In the fall and winter of 1540 Coronado was in the vicinity of Tiguex, not far from the present town of Bernalillo, and on April 23 of the following year he undertook the search for Quivira, about which the natives had spoken. Marching across upper Texas and through Oklahoma, he entered eastern Kansas, but finding nothing by way of wealth to encourage further exploration he turned homeward. He and his army passed the winter of 1541–42 at Tiguex amid such suffering and discontent that they were all happy to leave the region on April 23, 1542. They arrived in Mexico a few months later.

Between Coronado's expedition and that of Oñate in 1598, the following entries were made into New Mexico: Fray Agustín Rodríguez, 1581; Antonio Espejo, 1582, an expedition sent to the relief of Rodríguez; Gaspar Castaño de Sosa, 1590, unauthorized; and Leyva de Bonilla and Antonio Gutiérrez de Humaña, 1593, also unauthorized.

The Coronado expedition had left four martyrs in New Mexico and vicinity: Fr. Juan de Padilla, the protomartyr of the United States, Quivira, 1542; Fr. Juan de la Cruz, Tiguex, 1542; Bro. Luis de Escalona, Pecos, 1542; Bro. Luis de Ubeda, Pecos, 1554. The Rodríguez expedition, 1581, left three martyrs.

On September 21, 1595, the viceroy of New Spain, Luis de Velasco, approved a contract with Juan de Oñate for the conquest and pacification of New Mexico, and after many delays and inspections the army started out from the mines of Casco, New Vizcaya, on August 1, 1597. It is principally in the inventories taken during the Ulloa and the Salazar inspections,[3] June, 1596-February, 1597, and September, 1597-February, 1598, respectively, that we find the meager information we possess concerning any possible sacred images carried on this expedition.

The decrees of inspection demanded the declaration by all persons going on the expedition of "all provisions, arms, munitions, horseshoes, iron articles, horses, mules, livestock and anything else they may be taking along and that may belong to them."[4] There must have been a practical understanding on what was meant by "anything else they may be taking along," for only in the Salazar inspection did very many persons declare anything of personal use. Most declarations during the Ulloa inspection end with such statements as "We are not listing other things for personal use." In the Salazar inspection a number of persons declared such items as bedding, books, household supplies, utensils, and the like. In neither inspection are any sacred images declared, which simply indicates that the inspectors did not wish to burden the inventories with a multiplicity of articles of personal use which would have no bearing on the fulfillment of the requirements of the Oñate contract. The closest article approximating a religious image mentioned in the inventories (and this is not an image in the meaning of the word here intended) is "a headdress of pearls, with a gold image of Our Lady" listed among the belongings of the wife of one of the captains.

The friars were beyond doubt supplied by the crown with all things necessary for the exercise of their ministry, including sacred images, as required by Article 26 of the royal ordinances for new colonizations and pacifications in new discoveries in the Indies issued at Bosque de Segovia on July 13, 1573. This was agreed to by the viceroy in the Oñate contract.[5]

In the itinerary of the expedition the following entry appears:

> On August 2 [1598], feast day of Portiuncula, after celebrating the Holy Jubilee in the church of the friars of St. Francis, who always carried it with them and who had said many masses along the route . . .[6]

This "church" was, of course, a portable, or field altar, which would be adorned with at least one image, a crucifix. As the ten friars accompanying the expedition were not taking along any articles of war, and were responsible only to their superiors in matters pertaining to their baggage and equipment, none of them made any declarations during the inspections.

In July, 1598, Oñate arrived with his army and colonists at the Tewa pueblo of Okhe, near the present-day town of Española. He called the settlement San Juan de los Caballeros, adding *de los Caballeros,* according to Villagrá, the soldier-poet of the expedition, "in memory of those noble sons who first raised in these barbarous regions the Bloody Tree upon which Christ perished for the redemption of mankind."[7] But "it is more likely that those who named the pueblo were thinking of St. John the Baptist as the ancient patron of the Knights of Malta."[8] At this place the first settlement and capital of Spanish New Mexico was established.

On August 23 of the same year a church edifice was started, and was completed in fifteen days, dedicatory ceremonies being held on the eighth of September. Thus, to St. John the Baptist belongs the honor of having been selected as the patron of the first church erected in New Mexico.

There is ample evidence in the inventories previously mentioned of the presence in the Oñate expeditionary force of craftsmen, such as carpenters and blacksmiths, stated specifically in one case and indicated in many others by the listing of tools and implements of every sort. It appears that almost every man was capable of shoeing his own horses, judging from the frequency with which the tools and materials for this operation were declared.

Villagrá, in his famous epic, makes direct

3. Hammond and Rey, *Oñate, Colonizer of New Mexico,* I, 94–168 and 199–308.

4. *Ibid.,* I, 210.

5. *Ibid.,* I, 46, 65.

6. *Ibid.,* I, 321–22.

7. *Historia de la Nueva México,* Canto 16.

8. Adams and Chávez *in* Domínguez, *The Missions of New Mexico, 1776,* n.6, p. 89.

reference to the craftsmanship of the Spaniards coming to New Mexico:

> These men fashion their own arms and all the accoutrements for their horses. They repair their arquebuses, fashioning for them beautiful stocks and boxes. They repair their own armor and shields, and adorn their helmets in beautiful manner. They are expert surgeons and treat the wounds of their comrades most skillfully.[9]

The poet also states that Oñate's men "do not possess a single article not of their own handiwork. . . ."

Again in Villagrá's poem, we find mention of three sacred images carried by members of the expedition. Upon the occasion of the departure of Fray Diego Márquez to Mexico, Oñate "presented his friend, as a token of his love, with a holy image . . . ; his sister . . . presented him with an image of the Christ child, a work of inestimable value."[10] There must have been many sacred images in the eighty-three wagons and carts which accompanied the soldiers and colonists.

Scarcely had the dedication of the new church been completed when the friars were assigned to their posts of labor for the conversion of the Indians. Although they entered immediately upon their duties, it is very unlikely that any churches were erected, with the exception of the one at San Juan.

So little progress was made in the economic and religious order that during these first years it was a question whether New Mexico should be retained, or given up as an unprofitable possession. The harvest of souls had been small, while the hardships and expenses incident to the transportation of supplies over the long wagon trails from Mexico presented almost insurmountable difficulties. No gold or silver had been discovered, and the barren expanses were anything but inviting. Conditions became so intolerable that in 1601 most of the colonists deserted. From the contradictory declarations of witnesses at various investigations, and from the reports of the colonists, the governor and the viceroy, it is very manifest that the situation in New Mexico was far from a happy one. The colonists accused the friars of neither trying to learn the Indian languages, nor making efforts to convert the natives; and some of the friars, in turn, charged the colonists with obstructing the work of the missionaries by their ill-treatment of the Indians. Affairs had come to such a pass that the viceroy, Montesclaros, declared to the king on October 28, 1605, that "I cannot help but inform your majesty that this conquest is becoming a fairy tale."[11]

Before August 20, 1599, the viceroy had given permission to the agents of Oñate in Mexico to recruit troops, this in answer to the governor's appeal for help. By August, 1600, the official inspection of these new soldiers and colonists had been completed. The expedition started out in early September, 1600, and reached San Gabriel, which had been established as the new capital a few months after the settlement at San Juan, on Christmas Eve of the same year. No sacred images were declared during the inspection above referred to, the closest article being "a banner with . . . two emblems of our Lady and Santiago."

Toward the last few months of 1608 matters took a turn for the better, conversions increased, and the crown decided to retain the region and further its exploration. By 1622 the number of friars had been increased to twenty-four, but aside from the activities of these missionaries nothing of any consequence had transpired in New Mexico. The economic life of the province was limited to a primitive sort of agriculture, stock raising, and the simplest kind of commerce. Even in La Villa Real de Santa Fe, the new capital established by Governor Peralta in 1610, there was almost a complete dependence upon artisan "floaters, who came and went with the mission supply caravans." Although there were what might be called jacks-of-all-trades among the original settlers, New Mexico was not colonized by skilled craftsmen as had been the major centers of Mexico and Peru, but with soldiers and stockmen, which accounts for the scarcity of artisans from the begin-

9. *Op. cit.,* Canto 20.
10. *Ibid.,* Canto 11.
11. Hammond and Rey, *op. cit.,* II, 1009.

ning. The exigencies of life on what amounted to a frontier allowed little time for the development of craftsmanship other than that necessary to keep homes, tools and equipment in working condition.

The work of the missionaries continued to gain momentum, having received wonderful support in 1609-10, 1625, and 1628, when Fray Alonso Peinado, Fray Alonso de Benavides, and Fray Estevan de Perea, respectively, arrived with a total of sixty-four friars. The seventeenth century was indeed the Golden Age of the Franciscan missions in New Mexico.

About 1620 the first place of worship was erected in Santa Fe, the San Miguel Chapel,[12] built across the Santa Fe River in the section still known as *el barrio de Analco*, *analco* being the Aztec for "across the river." This chapel was for the use of various Indians of different origin, both Mexican and New Mexican.

When Fr. Benavides arrived in 1625 as custodian of the New Mexico missions, he deplored the fact that the only place of worship for the Spaniards of the capital was a crude *xacalón,* or mud hut. He therefore set about to erect a satisfactory church structure, which, completed in 1626, was dedicated to Our Lady of the Assumption. Around 1650 it was changed to Our Lady of the Immaculate Conception. This structure, known as La Parroquia, was completely demolished during the revolt of 1680, and was not rebuilt until 1714-17, and is now under the patronage of St. Francis of Assisi. Hence, the existing old sanctuary behind the rear wall of the cathedral is of the latter date.[13]

It is to the *xacalón* that Fr. Benavides refers in the following lines:

There spread among them [the Apache Vaqueros] the report and fame of the great beauty [of] and reverence for an image of the death of our Lady which I had placed in a chapel in the church in the villa of Santa Fe, where the Spaniards worshipped.[14]

The image mentioned is the same one today venerated in the cathedral in Santa Fe known as *La Conquistadora,* and listed in the following record of "Supplies for Benavides and companions going to New Mexico, 1624-1626": "Two figures of Christ, on wooden crosses. . . ." "Five oil painted images. . . ." "Another box . . . in which was packed the Virgin."[15]

This record of eight images is the best of any before the rebellion of 1680.

From about 1625 on, some of the missions set up schools and workshops where the Indians were taught reading, writing, music, and the manual arts. This was done on the initiative of the friars, for the civil authorities had done practically nothing to comply with the provisions of the Oñate contract, which, among other instructions, contained the following: "You shall charge the Spaniards to teach the Indians how they may assist and become useful in the . . . preservation of the Spanish organization. Do it in such a way that, upon learning the trades, they may apply themselves and attract others to them."[16] The Indians were soon to take over a good part of what little manufacturing was done in colonial New Mexico. It is a regrettable fact that in their zeal to Christianize the Indians the friars so neglected the colonists that craftsmanship degenerated and illiteracy became common among the latter. Santa Fe was the only town at this time in New Mexico, and here at least there is a 1639 record of one Rodrigo Lorenzo, a silversmith by trade.[17] There may have been silver to work, but "no iron has been sent since 1628."

A statement of the ornaments and other things to be given to each friar priest when leaving for New Mexico, dated April 30, 1631, lists "An oil painting," and for every five friars "two carved images of Christ."[18]

12. *See* Stubbs and Ellis, *Archaeological Investigations at the Chapel of San Miguel, passim.*

13. *See* Chávez, *Our Lady of the Conquest,* Chap. III.

14. Hodge, Hammond, and Rey, *Fray Alonso de Benavides' Revised Memorial of 1634,* p. 91.

15. *Ibid.,* p.121.

16. Hammond and Rey, *op. cit.,* I, 67.

17. Hackett, *Historical Documents,* III, 72.

18. Scholes, "The Supply Service of the New Mexico Missions in the Seventeenth Century," *New Mexico Historical Review,* V, 1 (January, 1930), 103.

The Oñate expedition and the Benavides supply train had brought some images, but considering that thirty-four Indian missions had been established up to 1631, it may be said that during the first half of the seventeenth century New Mexico did not have nearly enough images to satisfy the requirements of either the missions or the colonists.

To meet the need for sacred images, and apparently of a type to cover large spaces, paintings were executed in Mexico on animal skins of both Mexican and New Mexican origin, and by men of more than ordinary skill. These early paintings were done with the same earth, clay and vegetable pigments used later by the makers of folk images, but not in the tempera medium. Due to the absence of documentary materials, skin paintings constitute one of the problems of New Mexican sacred art. Exactly where and by whom they were painted are questions which cannot be categorically answered with the facts at hand.

Beyond the steady efforts of the missionaries, the seventeenth century offered little to lift the spirits of the colonists. Bitter relations between the clergy and the civil authorities developed early, directly traceable to differences of opinion regarding the division of authority.[19] The first quarter of the century cradled the relations referred to, and their evil effects were to be felt throughout the fifty-five years that remained of the century to Spanish domination. During the years 1639–41 the province was on the verge of civil war, and the turbulent administrations of López de Mendizabal, 1659–61, and Peñalosa Briceño y Berdugo, 1661–64, only added fuel to the fires of discontent.

In the area of secular education all the energies of the missionaries were directed toward teaching the Indians, and the Spanish were so ignored that illiteracy and ignorance were the dominant notes of the society of the time.

The few pitiful advantages won during these days were violently dislocated by the visitation of a great famine in 1670, when half the population, both Indian and Spanish, fought off starvation only by resorting to the extreme of eating roasted hides and straps with corn, herbs and roots. The next year a plague of some kind carried off many people and animals, and in 1672 the Apaches sacked and outraged the province from one end to the other.

It was in this same year, 1672, that the first inventories of church furnishings in New Mexico were taken. "Although the lists we have represent comparatively few [nine] establishments and are often tantalizingly incomplete or obscure, they are undoubtedly typical enough of the situation in the province as a whole."[20] The inventories list specifically a total of 9 paintings on canvas, fourteen figures in the round, and 1 painting on copper. All three of these classes are represented by entries reading "many" in several cases. In one church only the word "images" is used, and in another "painted retablos." As will be seen from the large number of images destroyed, mutilated and recovered after the revolt of 1680, the situation with regard to sacred images in the mission churches seems to have been somewhat satisfactory at this time.

---

19. Analogous situations existed throughout the Spanish and French colonies during the years of settlement.

20. Scholes and Adams, "Inventories of Church Furnishings in Some of the New Mexico Missions," *Dargan Historical Essays*, p. 29. *See also* Appendix C. Distribution of Images in the Inventories of 1672.

2. SACRED IMAGES AND the PUEBLO REVOLT OF 1680

ON AUGUST 10, 1680, a well-organized revolt of the Indians exploded with frightening fury and dismal effects. The Spanish residents of the outlying settlements were taken by complete surprise, and most of them were massacred without being given an opportunity to defend themselves. Four hundred Spaniards, including twenty-one Franciscans, were killed.

The Pueblo Indians had long resented being exploited by the Spanish citizens, and the rebellion of the natives was recognized as a serious threat as early as 1601. On September 7 of this year, Fray Francisco de San Miguel, the vice-commissary for New Mexico, testified before the lieutenant governor concerning the discontent that prevailed among both the Indians and the Spanish. After reciting the grievances of both peoples, he stated that he had "learned that the Indians, in view of the fact that the Spaniards have so few weapons, are daily plotting to fall upon them, waiting only for an opportune moment."[1] It appears from the testimony of Fray Francisco and other witnesses that every injustice had been practiced upon the Indians by the Spanish inhabitants, and this treatment continued up until the day of the revolt.

The survivors of the massacre of August 10, under the leadership of Governor Antonio de Otermín, were forced to make plans to abandon the province in view of their hopeless situation. By August 15 Santa Fe was under siege, with some one thousand Spaniards huddled in the capital. Less than one hundred were men capable of bearing arms. Another large group, including hundreds of women and children, had abandoned Isleta the day before and had started out on their long and arduous march to the south. Mile by mile they plodded along, most of them on foot, the few on horseback being men at arms disposed in such a way as best to protect the refugees from Indian attack. After fighting their way out of the capital, the Santa Fe group followed under similar conditions, finally reaching El Paso del Norte, some three hundred miles away. El Real de San Lorenzo, near El Paso, present-day Juárez, Mexico, became the temporary capital of New Mexico. When muster rolls were taken as the survivors staggered into the settlement, many appeared in starving condition and without a single article of personal possession. Three men, described in the record as over eighty years of age, passed muster on foot, naked, and with only a weapon to show for a lifetime of struggle with the rough forces of living on the frontiers of New Spain.

Here is a picture of the region in the wake of the revolt:

The condition of the province . . . now beggared description. From Taos to Isleta, a distance of over fifty leagues, the whole country, with the exception of Santa Fe, was devastated and depopulated. The estancias and haciendas of the Spanish settlers had been robbed both of household goods and of the horses and cattle in the fields, while many of the houses had been destroyed by fire. The churches, where not

---

1. Hammond and Rey, *Oñate, Colonizer of New Mexico,* II, 674.

burned, had been stripped of their sacred vessels, robbed of their ornaments, and in every way as completely and foully desecrated as Indian sacrilege and indecency could suggest. . .[2]

At the time of the revolt, the Indian chiefs had ordered the destruction of every vestige of Christianity and of Spanish civilization:

> . . . The rebels all remained masters of the entire kingdom; and as soon as the Spaniards were all gone out from it Po-pé [the Indian leader] gave orders, under pain of death to those who did not obey, that all of the men, women, and children should take off the crosses and rosaries which they might have and should break them in pieces or burn them; that no one should speak the name of Jesus and Mary, nor invoke the saints. . .[3]

A number of sacred images and articles survived the storm: some recovered by the retreating Spaniards, some hidden by faithful Indians, others retained by the rebels subsequent to the departure of the refugees after the former had made a systematic examination of the churches and homes.

On September 29 and October 2, 1680, near La Salineta and not far from the present city of El Paso, muster rolls were taken of the survivors. A complete inventory of all personal possessions carried by the refugees was made, attention being paid almost exclusively to personal arms. In the 166 entries, embracing 1,946 soldiers, servants, women, children and Indian allies, not one religious article is mentioned. Unquestionably, many of the refugees salvaged some of their images and other religious articles, not only of this group, but also of those who crossed into Nueva Vizcaya at another point and who were not listed in the muster rolls.[4]

Governor Otermín reported that on the twenty-fourth of August the retreating Spaniards arrived

> . . . at the pueblo of Santo Domingo. . . . The church and convent were closed, and upon investigation we found the images and altars as they had been left.[5]

The desecrations that took place during the course of the uprising are pictured in the following eyewitness account:

> ". . . they set fire to the holy temples and images, mocking them with their dances and making trophies of the priestly vestments and other things belonging to divine worship. Their hatred and barbarous ferocity went to such extremes that in the pueblo of Sandia images of the saints were found among excrement. . . ."[6]

This had taken place on the twenty-sixth of the preceding August, further described by Otermín:

> The images had been taken from the church and on the altar there was a full-length figure of Saint Francis with the arms hacked off by an axe.[7]

Three unsuccessful attempts to reconquer New Mexico were made: Governor Otermín, 1681; Governor Reneros de Posada, 1688; Governor Jironza Petriz de Crúzate, 1689.

The expedition of Otermín, while not accomplishing its purpose, did reap an abundant harvest of sacred images and religious articles, recovered in various ways and places along the line of march. A few examples will suffice: On the twenty-ninth of November the army reached the pueblo of Socorro, where

> On entering the plaza . . . there was found the entire thigh, leg and foot of a holy image of Christ in one piece, all the rest of the divine image being burned to charcoal and ashes; also some bases of images and many pieces of burned crosses.[8]

2. Hackett and Shelby, *Revolt of the Pueblo Indians of New Mexico*, I, lii-liii.

3. Fr. Escalante's letter to Fr. Morfi, in Twitchell, *The Spanish Archives of New Mexico*, II, 779, 272–73.

4. We know that one Josefa Sambrano de Grijalba carried an image of the Virgin with her on the retreat. See p. 16. Also, among the friars who escaped was one who carried with him to Mexico City an image afterwards called *Nuestra Señora de la Macana. See* Barreiro, *Ojeada sobre Nuevo Méjico,* p. 6, n. 1; also Hackett, *Historical Documents,* III, 495.

5. *Ibid.,* III, 15.

6. Hackett and Shelby, *op. cit.,* I, 177–78.

7. *Ibid.,* III, 26.

8. *Ibid.,* III, 205.

On December 5, the church and convent at Isleta were found burned, with all crosses down throughout the pueblo. On the ninth a bronze crucifix was recovered here, and a statue of Our Lady was found at Alameda. Between the fifth and the twentieth many religious articles, some valuable chalices, and images of various kinds were recovered at the two pueblos mentioned and at Sandía.

Otermín's attempt to reconquer New Mexico was both unsuccessful and costly. The images and other articles of church usage mentioned were only a few of those recovered by Otermín, and there was still much church property to be located. It remained for Don Diego de Vargas Zapata y Lujan Ponce de León to meet successfully the challenge to save New Mexico for the Spanish empire.

Vargas set out from El Paso del Norte with his army on August 21, 1692, and after a hard march, and without encountering any resistance, he drew up to the walls of Santa Fe in the early morning of September 13. The Indians who now occupied the former capital were hostile from the beginning; and after repeated supplications to surrender the city peacefully failed to reveal any disposition on their part to do so, Vargas laid down an ultimatum. By four o'clock in the afternoon the natives agreed to submit, so Vargas ordered them to hang crosses around their necks and to set up a large cross in the middle of the patio. The next day, which was the feast of the Exaltation of the Holy Cross, Vargas took formal possession of the Villa. During the negotiations with the Indians Vargas had repeatedly displayed the figure of Our Lady of Remedies on his banner. This royal standard, carried by Vargas throughout his two campaigns, was the same one used by Oñate when he founded the colony in 1598. It had been kept in Santa Fe and carried out in the retreat of 1680.

On the day following the surrender of the capital the first recovery of religious articles by the Vargas expedition took place when the leader of the Tewas, Tanos and Picurís presented to the general a number of items, including a small silver image of Christ and one

of Our Lady of Guadalupe on silk.[9] At Zuñi, on November 11, the Spaniards recovered two bronze figures of Christ on wooden crosses, a carved crucifixion with St. Francis Capuchin at the foot, a painting of St. John the Baptist, and several articles of brass, silver and rock crystal.[10]

On November 21, the Indian governor of Aguatuvi, the most eastern of the Moqui pueblos of Arizona, told Vargas how his tribesmen "had slain all the missionaries and settlers they could lay hands on, had burned the churches, thrown down all images of Christ, the Virgin, and the saints, . . . had made shirts, ribbons, waists, and jackets out of the sacred decorations and vestments; had profaned and destroyed the sacred vessels; . . ."[11]

Writing from El Paso on January 2, while preparing to return to New Mexico with more colonists, Vargas stated:

> It is my wish, with those with whom I enter, that they should first and foremost, personally build the Church and holy temple, setting up in it before all else, the patroness of the said kingdom and villa, who is the one that was saved from the ferocity of the savages, her title being Our Lady of the Conquest. . .[12]

About the middle of December, 1693, Vargas was back in Santa Fe, and among other projects he ordered the rebuilding of the ruined hermitage of San Miguel, just outside the walls of the Villa, in order to provide a sanctuary for ". . . Our Lady of the Conquest, . . . who was enclosed in a wagon and that if our Lady came they were obliged to provide a house for her."[13] The Virgen del Rosario, called *La Conquistadora*, now in the north chapel of the Cathedral of Saint Francis in Santa Fe, is the image referred to. Tradi-

9. Vargas' Campaign Journal, in A.G., *Audiencia de Guadalajara*, Legajo 139. Trans. by J. Manuel Espinosa, *First Expedition of Vargas into New Mexico*, p. 103.

10. *Ibid.,* pp. 201–03.

11. Espinosa, *Crusaders of the Rio Grande*, pp. 98–99.

12. Vargas' Campaign Journal, *op. cit.,* p. 116.

13. San Miguel Chapel: Original, ca. 1620; destroyed, 1640; rebuilt, 1650; destroyed, 1680; rebuilt, 1710, probably a complete new structure.

tion always held this to be so, and now, as so often happens, folklore has been verified:

> Without any doubt, the image treasured in the Santa Fe Parroquia from time immemorial, in whose honor a yearly celebration has been most faithfully kept because of the popular belief that it was brought by de Vargas at the time of the Reconquest, is the very same one which the Rosary Confraternity venerated at San Lorenzo [near El Paso]. The tradition that claims that she came with de Vargas is correct, but the *Reconquistador* himself tells us that this was but a return of a Queen to her former throne, from which she had been rescued from the fury of the Indian rebels.[14]

La Conquistadora had been brought to Santa Fe in 1625 by Fr. Alonso de Benavides, and enthroned as *Nuestra Señora de la Asunción* in the parish church. When the Spaniards retreated from Santa Fe on August 21, 1680, one Josefa Sambrano de Grijalba carried away the image in her arms.[15] At El Real de San Lorenzo the refugees had erected a chapel in her honor.[16]

On May 27–28, 1694, Vargas questioned a captive Jémez Indian concerning the burial place of Father Juan de Jesús, who had been martyred there in 1680, and the whereabouts of the religious articles and furniture of the former mission. The prisoner informed him that "a former governor of Jémez, now dead, had a box full of religious articles, but that the church bells, statues, and religious ornaments had been burned by order of certain Tewa leaders who had passed through the pueblo at the time of the uprising."[17]

In March, 1696, a few of the pueblos again revolted against Spanish authority. Although the rebellion was abortive, many acts of violence against church property took place. One of the first incidents was the stoning of the image of St. Lawrence at Picurís. The sacred vessels and ornaments of the convent at San Juan were saved on June 5, and on the following day the church at San Ildefonso was found burned. On the seventh it was discovered that the sacred vessels and the ornaments of the mission at Nambé had been carried away and

the convent sacked. Among the items saved was an image of Our Lady of the Immaculate Conception which had stood on the main altar. It was undamaged, and was removed for safekeeping to the mission at Santa Cruz.

On September 3, Miguel Saxette, the Indian governor of San Juan, reported to Vargas that the brothers Antonio and Lorenzo, the latter governor of Picurís, had all the religious articles of Picurís, and Vargas ordered that they be brought to him.

On September 24 Vargas received a number of religious articles from a former sacristan at Taos, including an oil painting of Our Lady of Aránzazu.[18]

It is remarkable that so many articles of church furniture, vestments and sacred vessels were recovered after the rebellion, particularly in the light of such information as the following:

> Being asked why they so blindly burned the images, crosses, temples and other things of divine cult, he said: "That the said Indian *Popé* went down in person and in company with *Xaca* and Chato, of the pueblo of Taos, and other captains and authorities, . . . and at every *pueblo* he went to he commanded them to immediately break up and burn the images of the Holy Christ and of the Virgin Mary, and those of other saints, crosses and all other things touching Christianity and to burn the temples, break the bells. . . ." etc.[19]

Whether because of superstitious fear, or because of a degree of attachment to the Catholic faith on the part of some of them, it seems that the Indians had to be ordered by their leaders to destroy the material manifestations of Christianity. The fact is that much was recovered, proving that enthusiasm for the destruction of sacred images and other religious

---

14. Chávez, *Our Lady of the Conquest*, p. 33.

15. Chávez, "La Conquistadora is a Paisana," *El Palacio*, (October, 1950), 301.

16. *Loc. cit.*

17. Vargas' Campaign Journal, *op. cit.*, pp. 185-86.

18. Of Basque origin, this Marian advocation enjoyed high favor at the time New Mexico was colonized.

19. *See* Twitchell, *Spanish Archives of New Mexico*, II, 63–64.

articles was not as universal as some writers imply. However, had it not been for the waves of mutilation and destruction which accompanied the revolts of 1680 and 1696, New Mexico today would be immeasurably richer in antique church furnishings, for many of the works destroyed or carried out by the refugees might have been of high artistic quality.

By the middle of November, 1696, peace reigned again over the New Mexico missions and settlements. The economic life of the colony depended upon the re-establishment of agriculture, cattle and sheep-raising, the various crafts, and other essential pursuits. Craftsmanship had been helped somewhat back in 1694 when on June 23 new colonists had arrived from Mexico City, among whom were many heads of families practiced in the useful trades.[20]

It appears that in the waning days of the seventeenth century the Indians of New Mexico still predominated in the practice of the few arts and crafts which had been taught to them during the halcyon days of the Franciscan missions. The Spanish laity had been all but ignored in so far as instruction of any kind was concerned. During the great days of the missions and from the very beginning of the new colony established after the reconquest, the New Mexican, as Dickey has said, "had to be self-reliant, for he was the most neglected individual in New Mexican society."

The great Diego de Vargas died at Bernalillo on April 8, 1704, ending one of the most historic periods in the annals of New Mexico. His last will and testament is concerned with sacred images, for of his many personal possessions he left to his American-born sons Don Juan and Don Alonzo de Vargas "the banners of Anselm and Saint Michael the Great."

---

20. *See* Vargas' Campaign Journal, *op. cit.,* 189, n. 31.

3. the eighteenth century and the advent of folk image-making

THE 1700's in New Mexico were years of continued discomfort for the colonials, if not so much so as the joyless days of exploration, settlement, retreat and reconquest. The economy of the province was in a far from satisfactory condition, a fact brought into focus by a petition dated May 8, 1705, asking the governor to apply to the viceroy "for assistance for the inhabitants of New Mexico."

By 1700 the Pueblo Indians were at peace with their Spanish neighbors, but the Plains Indians were to become a worse scourge than any of the sedentary tribes had ever been. The continuous depredations of the Apaches, Utes, Navahos and Comanches came to bear so heavily on the settlements that they brought about conditions of general poverty. This is an important fact to bear in mind when accounting for the advent of folk craftsmanship in the area of religious images around the third quarter of the century.

Echoing the general trend throughout the Spanish-Colonial empire, changes of consequence were taking place in the political, economic and religious order. Permanent, self-supporting settlements were emphasized. The crusading zeal of the sixteenth and seventeenth centuries was being dissipated by a growing secular spirit. Toward the end of the century, in 1781, the number of missions was reduced to twenty by order of the governor, effecting a consolidation which, although opposed by the Franciscans, seemed to make for better organization.

Just as significant to the future history of the province were the knocks of strangers at her northern and eastern gates. As early as 1703, a group of twenty Canadians left the Illinois country with the purpose of investigating the mineral wealth of New Mexico. Between 1718 and 1739, French trappers from Louisiana made a number of attempts to reach New Mexico, and in the latter year the Mallet brothers succeeded. The many tribes of hostile Indians served as barriers between the two areas, as did the constant alertness of the Spanish authorities in their determination to keep all foreigners out of the northern outposts of New Spain. In spite of these obstacles, attempts continued to be made, and in 1748 a French party of thirty-one reached the borders of present-day New Mexico. During the following fifty years many French groups either went to Santa Fe or were taken there after being discovered in Spanish territory.

The dedication of officialdom to the task of bringing about a more stable disposition and distribution of urban life is seen in the steady organization of new communities. In 1706, two years after the death of Vargas, Governor Cuervo y Valdez sent some forty families to establish a settlement near or perhaps on the site of the hacienda of Don Luis Carabajal, which had been destroyed at the time of the revolt of 1680. Settlers for the new town were from near Bernalillo, and they were only too happy to make a change of residence due to the constant menace of hostile Apaches from the nearby Sandía Mountains. The new settlement was called La Villa de San Francisco Xavier de Alburquerque, the first part of the name inspired by San Francisco Xavier del

Bosque Grande, by which name the vicinity of the new town was known, and the last part honoring the viceroy, the Duke of Alburquerque. San Felipe Apostol appears in the registers as patron from August 9, 1709, to January, 1711; San Francisco Xavier again from January 8, 1711, to April, 1777, from which time on San Felipe Neri appears. The latter has been the patron ever since.[1]

The older towns, Santa Fe, Bernalillo and Santa Cruz became the important centers. The sites of old haciendas were settled, as were also some of the old missions. After 1763, international problems on the northern frontier and the permanent menace of the Plains Indians deterred the establishment of new communities or an extension of the activities of the missionaries.

Culturally, the history of the eighteenth century in New Mexico was not very different from that of the seventeenth. Social and religious activities continued as before. The labors of the field and household were relieved by church festivals, Masses, baptisms, marriages, public prayers, religious processions, military parades, wakes and burials. Fiestas, with their accompanying entertainments, such as dancing and singing popular songs and ballads, made up the lighter but important side of the same old way of life. The yearly caravans to Chihuahua to barter, trade and buy at the January fair returned not only with foreign goods, but brought into New Mexico the little news received from the outside world, with the exception of those items of information contained in the royal and viceregal decrees and correspondence which periodically arrived. Generations of isolation were fixing the customs, habits and folk traditions of the people.

During the first years after the reconquest the need for sacred images again manifested itself. Once reconquered and resettled, the province no longer elicited either appreciable interest or reasonable support from the viceregal government. The citizenry found itself obliged to work out its own economic salvation, and, incident to this effort, craftsmanship of an altogether folk order developed under

the tutelage of the mother of invention. This is plainly evident in the tools and household furnishings of the eighteenth century which can be seen today in homes, private collections and museums.

The problem of supplying the churches and chapels with images, vestments and other appurtenances of the Divine Office was even greater than in 1630. On January 7, 1706, Fray Juan Álvarez, Custodian of the New Mexico missions, sent a lengthy report to the governor, from which the following is taken:

> That I . . . recognize the very needy condition of the poor missions of this kingdom. I see that, although the father custodians who were my predecessors asked for succor, they were not able to obtain it because the governors were concerned deeply with nothing save their own lawsuits; . . . I am obliged to make representation to your lordship concerning that which I consider so essential, . . .
>
> That, it being the will of God, our Lord, that this kingdom, lost in the year 1680, should be restored in the year 1692, his Majesty conceded, and . . . the Count of Galve, as his agent, gave a replenishment of ornaments, chalices, and bells for the decent equipment of some of the newly-restored missions. After the missionary religious had been stationed in them came the fatal year of 1696 in which revolts again occurred among the apostate Indians . . . , fifteen pueblos in all. They took the lives of five religious, . . . and with mortal hatred for our holy faith, not only burned and desecrated the temples, but tore down and broke the ornaments, sacred vessels, altars, images, and bells, so that it has been impossible to restore any of them.
>
> I beseech and supplicate your lordship to look upon this cause with your customary Catholic zeal, . . . so that these poor missions may be supplied with the ornaments . . . and images which are customarily provided. . .[2]

In a declaration dated at Santa Fe five days after the above report, Fr. Álvarez stated that he had visited all the missions in order to have a first-hand knowledge of their needs. He re-

1. *See* Adams and Chávez *in* Domínguez, *The Missions of New Mexico, 1776*, p. 146, n.3.
2. Hackett, *Historical Documents*, III, 369–71.

ported twenty-three churches most inadequately equipped insofar as vestments, ornaments, chalices, bells and sacred images were concerned.[3]

Some images—it is not possible to determine the number—were brought into New Mexico between the year of the Vargas reconquest of 1692 and the revolt of 1696, as indicated by Fr. Álvarez' statement. There could not have been many, for the revolt of 1696 affected only fifteen out of twenty-six missions then in operation, yet all of them were short of, and four were totally without ornaments. Also included in the list of those missions in great need of images and ornaments were the faithful pueblos of Pecos, Tesuque, San Felipe, Santa Ana, and Zía, and the Spanish chapels at Alameda, Bernalillo, Santa Cruz and Santa Fe. The dearth of church furniture was such that

> In some of the poorer churches there is only one cross, the poor religious making use of some which have been painted by the Indians according to their style so that they may have some appearance of decency. . . . Some of them, in fact, who knew the adornments used in past times, note that the mass is now said with dilapidated ornaments, and that the churches, although properly clean, are without ornaments.[4]

It may be that Fr. Álvarez' zeal led him to exaggerate the needs of the missions; otherwise it would appear that very few images were brought into the province between 1692 and the time of the report, 1706. If the chapels and churches lacked adornments, we can imagine what the homes of the people must have been like in this regard, excepting, of course, the habitations of people of some means whose worldly possessions were enough to require the execution of a will.

Recognizing the great need for church furnishings, what was being done locally to supply them? There is no evidence whatever that the Indians turned out any church furniture beyond the making of crosses and the carving of such objects as altar railings. No flat paintings or statuary of a Christian character were executed by the Indians, in spite of their so-

called training in the workshops during the peak period of the missions. With the exception of paintings on skin, the images lost and those recovered during and after the revolts of 1680 and 1696 were unquestionably of Mexican origin, with a few coming from Spain.

The oft-stated opinion that the Franciscans were skilled wood-carvers who taught this art to the Spanish colonials is pure invention. There is no question that there were artisans of skill among the friars, for otherwise they could not have planned and supervised the building and maintenance of churches nor carried on instruction in the schools and workshops where the Indians were taught useful crafts, as is so often related in early records. With two unique and accidental exceptions, there is no evidence in surviving statuary that the friars carved images in the round. Every document and printed record examined relating to the work of the missionaries, from the foundation of the colony in 1598 to the time when the Franciscans started to leave New Mexico in 1817, points unmistakably to the conclusion that the friars did not have time either to paint or carve for the churches, and much less so for the public market, even though they may have had the training and the ability to do so. From the evidence we possess, there were many early paintings on hide, both in the homes of the people and in the churches and chapels.[5]

The Spanish Archives of New Mexico, catalogued in Vol. I of Twitchell's work bearing this title, contain 1,384 numbered entries. Of this total, 150 are mostly wills, with a few inventories of estates and proceedings for the settlement of estates, from the Vargas will of 1704 to one dated May 9, 1843. As only a total of 40 of the 150 wills or inventories listed in Vol. I of Twitchell and one will in Vol. II have been examined by the present au-

---

3. *Ibid.,* III, 371–78.

4. *Ibid.,* III, 370.

5. The clergy, it seems, only tolerated painted skins, for records of the missions now in the Chancery Office in Santa Fe, some dated as early as 1720, are bound in cuttings from them. Many of these cuttings are in good condition, which means that when cut they were in excellent state.

thor,[6] some lacunae may be filled by reading the voluminous materials contained in the 109 wills and inventories still unexplored.

Excepting the few entries in the church inventories taken in April 21–August 27, 1796, and June 5–July 28, 1806, Archive 1360 and 1993, respectively, of Twitchell, Vol. II, there is no evidence that either the civil or ecclesiastical authorities did other than ignore the religious folk art under their daily observation from the time of its appearance in the third quarter of the eighteenth century down to the very end of Mexican rule in 1846.

Sacred images of all kinds are frequently mentioned in the wills above referred to. Provision was made for the disposition of engravings, prints, paintings on skin, on buffalo hide, on canvas, on wood, crucifixes, images in the round, silver images of the saints, and rosaries:

Juan de Archiveque, Santa Fe, 1721;[7] "Eleven painted deerskins. Twenty painted hides." María de la Candelaria González,[8] Santa Fe, 1750: ". . . a *bulto* of Saint Anthony. . . . a *bulto* of Our Lady of the Pillar and a *retablo* of Our Lady of Remedies." María Garduño,[9] Santa Fe, 1752: ". . . twelve *santos* on paper, the rest on deerskin." Juana Galvana,[10] Santa Fe, 1753: "One Holy Child painted on wood, . . ." Miguel Lucero,[11] Albuquerque, 1766: "A wooden *bulto* of St. Joseph . . . A small wooden Christ . . ." Francisco Martín,[12] San Antonio del Embudo, 1767: "Four images on buffalo skin. A *bulto* of Our Lady of the Rosary."

Considering that one man possessed 31 painted skins in 1721, and assuming that they were not all recent acquisitions, we may conclude that the painting of sacred images on the skins of animals was just as extensive immediately after the reconquest of 1696 as it had been during the opening years of the seventeenth century. One thing is certain, that during both the seventeenth and eighteenth centuries there were many painted skins in service in New Mexico.

In the light of several documented facts, the Juan de Archiveque will of 1721 raises a number of questions. Archiveque was one of the survivors of the ill-fated La Salle expedition of 1687, who was in Santa Fe as early as 1697. After his death at the hands of the Pawnees on August 17, 1720, an inventory of his goods and chattels was made. Adolf F. A. Bandelier, the great ethno-historian, after a reading of certain *Diligencias matrimoniales* in the archives of the pueblo of Santa Clara in June, 1888, and of Archives Nos. 6 and 13 of Twitchell, Vol. I, then in the Office of the Surveyor General in Santa Fe, wrote that "We further gather that Archibeque . . . after leaving the military service, became a successful trader, extending his trading tours to Sonora and sometimes buying directly at the City of Mexico."[13]

The fact that Archiveque was a trader explains his possession of 31 painted skins. The statement that he extended his trading tours as far as Mexico City is provocative of thought on the origin of these skin paintings. Every kind of art work which came into New Mexico from the earliest days to well into the nineteenth century came from Mexico. Skins and hides were taken to Mexico from New Mexico throughout Spanish colonial times, buffalo hides being particularly well received in New Spain. Every one of the 26 old paintings on animal skins which exists today[14] is the work of artists of training and more than ordinary skill, whose work, if executed on wood or canvas would grace any church today. These paintings existed in quantity in New Mexico during the seventeenth and eighteenth centuries, 112 being listed in the inventories

---

6. Nos. 13, 48, 49, 88, 94, 101, 123, 124, 144, 154, 193, 197, 198, 344, 351, 359, 393, 452, 454, 458, 513, 530, 552, 559, 600, 604, 611, 626, 661, and 717, in the original Spanish as copied by Miss Carmen Espinosa. The Vargas will in Twitchell's translation. Nos. 56, 104, 177, 240, 244, 355, 373, 394, 399, 860, and 1202 in Ina Sizer Cassidy, "Santos and Bultos in the Spanish Archives," *El Palacio,* (February, 1952). No. 406 in Miss Espinosa's transcription of the original Spanish.

7. *S.A.D.I.,* Archive No. 13.

8. *Ibid.,* Archive No. 334.

9. *Ibid.,* Archive No. 351.

10. *Ibid.,* Archive No. 193.

11. *Ibid.,* Archive No. 454.

12. *Ibid.,* Archive No. 600.

13. *Nation,* August 30, 1888.

14. *See* Appendix G. Existing Paintings on Animal Skins.

of 1776,[15] and had their creators lived in New Mexico they unquestionably would not have limited their work to paintings on skin, but would have painted also on wood, which was plentiful. We know that existing paintings on skin were done with the same vegetable and earthen colors used by later folk artists in New Mexico, and that Mexican artists had these same materials at their disposal, although the early paintings on skin seem to be executed with a more opaque tempera than that used by the *santeros.* Domínguez reported in 1776 that several paintings on buffalo hide listed in his inventories were painted in oils.[16] A man of his background could probably tell oil from tempera, and if he was right about these oils on skin we have another argument for the Mexican origin of early skin paintings.

There is a fragment of a painting on wood in the Harwood Foundation at Taos (Pl. 8) inscribed SAN GERONIMO DOTOR. It is a good copy of an engraving by Justus Sadeler after an oil painting by Jacopo Palma the Elder, and is just another example of the great influence on the art of the Spanish colonies of the engravings of Central Europe. Although the paint is in fairly good condition this *retablo* is very old, possibly dating from as early as 1700, seventy-five years before the advent of the *santero.* The semicircular lunette, or shell, which decorates the top of the panel, so common to all European and Spanish-American art forms, is the earliest on a *retablo* found in New Mexico. The roundness of the figure of St. Jerome and the naturalistic landscape background are the most prominent characteristics of this panel which place it in a category quite removed from folk representations. This panel is executed in the same style and manner as old paintings on skin, and dates from the same general period, so it is concluded that it also is the work of a Mexican artist. It would not have been done in New Mexico for the same reasons advanced in the case of painted skins. This panel is unique in New Mexican art history.

In 1752 the first inkling of competition from the east in the sale of religious articles appeared. On August 6 of that year two French Canadians with nine horses loaded with bales of clothing and other goods arrived at the Pecos mission. Among the eighty-nine items listed in their invoice were "8 dozen crosses."[17]

In 1761 there was installed in the recently completed *Castrense,* or military chapel, in Santa Fe the famed altar-screen of Our Lady of Light, the patroness of the chapel. This reredos is the work of unknown Mexican artists, but it is supposed that they were from Mexico City, especially brought to Santa Fe for the work by Governor Francisco Marín del Valle, manifestly observing the indigence of the capital in matters related to church ornamentation. American occupation ended the glories of the *Castrense,* and the sale of the old chapel by Archbishop Lamy in 1859 marked the beginning of the neglect of its altar-screen. It remained hidden in a back room of the Cathedral of St. Francis until 1940, when it was called upon to grace the new church of Cristo Rey in Santa Fe. This reredos and the one done by a folk artist in the church at Laguna Pueblo are the two finest in all New Mexico.[18]

During the eighteenth century the need for sacred images in New Mexico among the laity, and to a lesser degree in the chapels and churches, was to some extent satisfied by the importation of small oil paintings on copper, tin, wood, canvas, and linen, coming in the caravans from Mexico. Religious paintings of all types were extraordinarily abundant in

15. Domínguez, *The Missions of New Mexico, 1776, passim.*

16. *Ibid.,* pp. 18, 184, 204.

17. Thomas, *The Plains Indians and New Mexico,* pp. 82, 98.

18. *See* Chávez, *La Conquistadora. The Autobiography of an Ancient Statue,* p. 95. The story of the altar-screen of Our Lady of Light may be read in: Adams, "The Chapel and Cofradia of Our Lady of Light in Santa Fe"; Eustis, "Eighteenth Century Catholic Stone Carvings in New Mexico"; Kelemen, "The Significance of the Stone Retable of Cristo Rey"; Stubbs and Ellis, *Archaeological Investigations;* and Von Wuthenau, "The Spanish Military Chapel in Santa Fe." For excellent reproductions of entire reredos and individual panels *see* Kelemen, *op. cit.,* and color restoration in Domínguez, *The Missions of New Mexico, 1776,* frontispiece.

Mexico during both the eighteenth and nineteenth centuries. "Every engraving that came to Mexico was copied in identical pictures turned out by the hundreds, filling the monasteries with lives of the saints."[19] The painters of these images frequently achieved masterpieces in miniature (Pls. 4 and 5). Paintings of this type, measuring an average of 5″ × 7″, reached New Mexico even before 1680, as shown by the inventories of 1672, but entered in quantity from around 1750 on. They were still coming in during the first quarter of the nineteenth century. Being executed on durable metal, many of these paintings have survived the years in excellent condition.

Sometime during the third quarter of the eighteenth century the first folk artists appear, following the example of their more learned brethren by copying directly from sophisticated models. A few outstanding examples of this early Humanist School of folk artists are: *Retablos: Our Lady of Solitude,* Taylor Museum; *St. Barbara,* Museum of New Mexico; *St. Rosalia of Palermo,* Wells Collection, Museum of New Mexico. *Bultos: The Holy Family,* St. Joseph (Pl. 9), *Our Lady of Solitude,* and *St. Michael,* all in the Gilberto Espinosa Collection; and *The Holy Family* of the Kleijkamp and Monroe Collection.

Establishment of the third quarter of the eighteenth century as the time when the first untrained artists started to work is not an arbitrary or a fancied conclusion, but one which is predicated on a number of known factors to be considered presently.

A view of the beginnings of religious folk craftsmanship in New Mexico is brought into better focus by information contained in the church inventories and other matters presented in the Domínguez report of 1776.[20] This report embraced an exceptionally detailed inventory of sacred images in the churches of twenty-two Indian pueblos and fourteen Spanish chapels and churches. A study of their distribution[21] and the observations of Fr. Domínguez about them is of primary consequence to this inquiry.

The large number of early folk-made images in the round leads to the opinion that the people first tried their hand at this type of representation rather than at the execution of flat paintings. A glance at the distribution of images in the Domínguez report shows the existence in 1776 of 321 flat paintings on various base materials. If we add to this total the 50 prints and 18 colored prints listed, we have 393 flat images as against 102 statues. As all images listed numbered 504, 77.81 per cent of the total was made up of flat representations. This is conspicuous evidence of the scarcity of statuary during the last half of the eighteenth century in New Mexico, which might explain the preponderance of early folk-made *bultos* and the efforts of the people to supply them.

A further indication of the need for statuary is found in the identification of 1 statue as having been fashioned by one Franciscan, and 7 by another, both friars doing their best to adorn the churches in their charge. Of the church at Nambé Fr. Domínguez writes: "Above the one [adobe table] on the Epistle side there is a poor niche . . . and in it a small image in the round which Fr. Toledo made . . . and it is ugly enough."[22] Describing the high altar at Santa Cruz: "The principal niche is in the first section, and there is a large image in the round of Our Lady of the Rosary in it . . . Fr. García made the image, and perhaps for the shame of her being so badly made they left the varnish on her face very red."[23] Two other images at Santa Cruz,[24] 2 at Taos, and 2 at Laguna[25] were also made by Fr. García. Of the ones at Taos Fr. Domínguez says: "And it is a pity that he should have used his labor for anything so ugly as the said works are—as bad as the ones mentioned at La Cañada."[26] The importance of these entries is that they supply documentary evidence of home craftsmanship applied to religious images as early as 1753 and 1765,

19. Toussaint, *Twenty Centuries of Mexican Art,* p. 70.
20. Domínguez, *op. cit.*
21. *See* Appendix D, Distribution of Images in the Inventories of 1776.
22. Domínguez, *op. cit.,* pp. 53–54.
23. *Ibid.,* pp. 73–74.
24. *Ibid.,* p. 75.
25. *Ibid.,* p. 184.
26. *Ibid.,* p. 104.

for Fr. Juan José Toledo was at Nambé between October 22, 1753, and October 24,
1755, and Fr. Andrés García was at Santa
Cruz between July 28, 1765, and May 19,
1768.

Although no specific mention is made in the
Domínguez report of any images executed by
the common people, there are very audible
sounds of the crude implements of the folk artist in a number of places. It is not only possible but very probable that Fr. Domínguez
had occasion to visit the homes of the people,
in spite of the fact that he does not give even
a casual notice of having done so. Assuming
that he did, still he would not feel constrained
to dwell upon the subject of home furniture, a
topic alien to the purposes of his visitation.
That he does not make any reference whatever to folk-made images in the homes might
suggest that folk craftsmen were not yet active in the year 1776. A number of observations by Domínguez could point to the oppo-
site position.

Of the images at San Juan he says: "During the time when . . . Junco[27] was missionary at this mission, a woman called Catarina
Pando gave this church the image of Jesus
Nazareno . . . and the image of Our Lady
of the Rosary . . . Both of them are so unworthy that they do not deserve the titles of
the Most Holy Personages they wish to represent. Therefore I ordered that they be con-
sumed by fire. . . .the St. John ["A small
St. John, old and unseemly."] . . . will go
into the fire immediately."[28] Fr. Domínguez
does not state that these "unworthy" images
were the handiwork of priests, and it is most
unlikely that they were, for the overworked
missionaries certainly had no time to be making images for the people. Where, then, did
the donor secure them? It would seem unrea-
sonable to fancy that they were importations,
for if they were as unattractive as Fr. Domínguez made them out to be, no merchant would
have bothered to cart them all the way from
even the nearest Mexican settlement. This entry, involving three images, is the strongest argument to support the opinion that folk

craftsmen were at work long before 1776, the
year of the Domínguez visitation.

Fr. Domínguez was not the first to order
the removal of undesirable images from the
churches. While at San Juan he listed "A pair
of cruets that Father Junco made out of silver
gewgaws collected from the settlers when the
Holy Bishop gathered up ugly images."[29]
Who were the authors of these "ugly images,"
existing in New Mexico seventeen years before the Domínguez visitation?

Describing the church at Santo Domingo
Fr. Domínguez writes: "The one [table] on
the right has a large oil painting on canvas in
a wooden frame of Our Lady of the Conception. This was painted at the said father's ex-
pense by an incompetent craftsman, but it
serves for devotional purposes. . . . There
is an image of Our Father St. Dominic on
the left-hand altar, all carved in wood and a
vara high. The natives of the pueblo bought
it. It is a product of this kingdom and by the
same hand that painted the above-mentioned
Immaculate Conception. And my statement
about the said painting will indicate that this
work is not very fine."[30] These two images
were "products of this kingdom" and by an
"incompetent craftsman"—in other words,
they were executed in New Mexico by an amateur, apparently a layman. Otherwise Fr. Domínguez probably would have hit upon the
name of the Franciscan author as he did in the
case of the images at Nambé, Santa Cruz,
Taos and Laguna.

Home craftsmanship is again indicated by
the case of an image at San Felipe: "The gos-
sipy vulgar herd have always considered St.
Philip the Apostle as the titular patron of
this mission. . . . A European citizen of this

27. Fr. José Eleuterio Junco y Junquera was at San Juan
between March 8, 1763, and August 8, 1770.

28. Domínguez, *op. cit.*, p. 86.

29. *Ibid.*, p. 87. The Holy Bishop referred to was probably Bishop Tamarón, who visited New Mexico in 1760. As
the first record of Fr. Junco's presence in New Mexico puts
him at San Felipe on October 29, 1762, there would seem
to be an error on the part of Domínguez as to the coinci-
dence of the time when Fr. Junco made the cruets and that
of the Bishop's action.

30. *Ibid.*, p. 133.

kingdom, called Don Bernardo Miera y Pacheco, supported this opinion by selling to the Indians of this pueblo . . . an image of the said Holy Apostle, a large carved statue in the round, which he made himself. And although it is not at all prepossessing, it serves the purpose. . . ."[31] Crude indeed, this image still stands in the central niche of the high altar at San Felipe.

At Nambé Fr. Domínguez wrote: "The one [altar] on the Gospel side has only a large painting on buffalo skin which represents Our Father St. Francis in the regional manner."[32] Of the 30 paintings on animal skin known to exist today, only 4 are the work of New Mexican *santeros,* and done in what might be called a "regional manner." The other 26 are executed in the traditional style, by artists of considerable schooling. The painting of St. Francis mentioned may have been the first on buffalo skin by a folk craftsman.

Instead of contradicting the judgment that religious folk-made images were first executed in New Mexico sometime during the third quarter of the eighteenth century, the information contained in the Domínguez report would seem strongly to support it.

The large-scale disappearance of paintings on animal skin from the churches and chapels of New Mexico took place between 1776 and 1796. The Domínguez report of 1776 lists 112 painted skins, whereas inventories of the churches taken in 1796 list 16, and by 1806 only 3 were left. Today there are only 4 skin paintings in service—1 at Santo Domingo, 1 at Laguna, and 2 at Galisteo.[33] Ninety-six of these paintings, or 85.96 per cent of the 1776 total, vanished from the churches within twenty years after the Domínguez visitation. It would thus appear that the good friar did more than order the burning of 3 "unworthy" *bultos.*

It should be stated that the church inventories of 1796 and 1806 cannot be relied upon, for in the case of several chapels and churches only the vestments and sacred vessels are listed, with no mention whatever of sacred images. Inventories were taken in twenty-two churches and chapels by Domínguez in 1776, whereas fifteen were examined in 1796, and only seven in 1806, and in only four of the 1806 inventories are any images listed.[34]

The source of paintings on animal skin is further clarified by an entry in the inventories of 1796, listing at Santa Cruz "6 framed paintings on calfskin of various saints."[35] The fact that these paintings were framed would indicate workmanship worthy of such attention, and as calfskin was never used in New Mexico as a base material it would seem that these images were executed in Mexico, as were paintings on buffalo and deerskin.

The making of folk representations of the saints was in full stride by the last quarter of the eighteenth century. This is amply documented in the 1796 inventories, which list *bultos, retablos* and reredos of folk execution. The following entry made at Santa Cruz is of very special interest: "There is also a wooden bier, painted, new, large, where is kept the image of Christ in the Sepulcher, which is very beautiful."[36] This image is still at Santa Cruz, and represents *santero* art at its best (Pl. 32). Fr. José Mariano Rosete, who signed the Santa Cruz inventory, states that the bier was new, which might infer that the figure of Christ was not new. In any case it was carved previous to 1796. This image of Christ is articulated, and was used to represent scenes of the Passion, as is borne out by the following entry: "A hewn cross, for [use in representing] the Descent."[37]

We may be certain that three of the "four reredos of wood painted with various images"[38] are the ones still at Santa Cruz, and these also are the work of New Mexico folk craftsmen.

31. *Ibid.,* p. 160.
32. *Ibid.,* p. 53.
33. *See* Appendix F, Paintings on Animal Skins Listed in Three Church Inventories.
34. *See* Appendix E, Distribution of Statues, Oil Paintings and Paintings on Wood in Three Church Inventories.
35. *S.A.M.N.M.,* Archive No. 1360.
36. *Loc. cit.*
37. *Loc. cit.*
38. *Loc. cit.*

Of the inventories taken in 1796 only those at the Church of the Holy Cross, Santa Cruz, and at San Francisco, Santa Fe, were carefully done. No mention of the famed reredos in the *Castrense* is made, which shows how slipshod were these inventories. In all the inventories a distinction is always made between *retablos* (paintings on wood) and *lienzos* (paintings on canvas). Very few sophisticated paintings on wood have come down to us, while folk paintings on wood exist today by the hundreds. It is concluded, therefore, that most of the *retablos* listed in the inventories were of folk workmanship.

The closing years of the eighteenth century showed the offensive results of two hundred years of royal and viceregal neglect of all education in New Mexico, during which time New Spain witnessed the consistent practice and ex-perienced the continuous enjoyment of all the arts and crafts. None of these were passed on to New Mexico by action of the viceregal authorities until 1805, when two master weavers, Ignacio and Juan Bazán, were sent to teach their trade.

In the light of the conditions which maintained in New Mexico from the establishment of the colony down to the opening years of the nineteenth century, it is difficult to understand why New Mexico continued to hold its attraction as "the land of enchantment," established in 1536 when Cabeza de Vaca wandered into Culiacán burdened with his notorious yarn. Two hundred and seventy-one years later it remained only for the citizens of the United States to read the inviting pages of Pike to move westward in search of another Cíbola.

4. the years of transition

IN REPLY to a request made in a royal order of June 21, 1802, Governor Chacón reported on the twentieth of August of the same year:

> With respect to the arts and trades, it may be said with propriety that there are none in this province, there being no apprenticeship, official examination for master-workmen, any formality of trades-unions, or other things customary in all parts, but necessity and the natural industry of these inhabitants has led them to exercise some, for example weaving in wool, shoemaking, carpentry, tailoring, blacksmithing, and masonry, in which nearly all are skilled. . . .[1]

The province of New Mexico, then, still depended upon home craftsmanship for all essential tasks. Although the folk art and craft of sacred image-making was then in full stride it was not mentioned in the Governor's report.

The nineteenth century opens with an increase in the number of foreign visitors, which was to transform social, economic and political patterns in New Mexico and to determine the course of her subsequent history. A French Creole by the name of Batiste La Lande made the first expedition to Santa Fe from United States territory, having been sent out in 1804 to look into the possibilities of trade. In 1808 James Purcell, a Kentuckian, came to Santa Fe to negotiate agreements for a band of Mandan Indians. A carpenter by trade, Purcell found conditions so much to his liking that he remained in the capital, pursuing his craft with great success. His case emphasizes anew the ever-present dearth of artisans in New Mexico, a condition observed with annoying monotony since the times of the reconquest.

The visit to New Mexico of Zebulon Montgomery Pike in 1806–07, whose report supplied the first authentic information on the Southwest to the United States government, offers some testimony of interest. While in Santa Fe, Pike noted that although manufacturing was carried on to a reasonable extent, it was mostly in the hands of Indians, since, as he said, the Spaniards preferred to give their time to agriculture. Generations of necessary concentration had not implanted in the New Mexican a predilection for agricultural pursuits. The fact is that he was still struggling against frontier conditions to meet the exigencies of living. We should not lose sight of the fact that New Mexico was still a frontier when United States troops entered Santa Fe in 1846. It had been the northernmost outpost of New Spain since the days of the first colony, and in point of actuality it was still a frontier up to the closing years of the nineteenth century when the Plains Indians were finally subdued and placed within the boundaries of reservations.

On March 5, 1807, Pike stopped at the Indian pueblo of Santo Domingo, where he visited the church and had words of praise for the images there. Two days later he arrived in Albuquerque, where he examined the rectory of San Felipe de Neri. Here the sacred images excited his appreciation. All of the images commented on by him were importations from Mexico. Doubtless, Pike saw many folk-made images, but he made no mention of them.

---

1. *S.A.M.N.M.*, Archive No. 1670a.

The *Grito de Dolores* of September 15, 1818, the first move toward Mexican independence, was scarcely audible in New Mexico, and the issues involved were neither well known nor understood there. New Mexico awaited the results of the revolution with only casual interest, but on January 6, 1822, inspired by the authorities, Santa Fe celebrated the success of the revolution with public demonstrations, speeches, processions, artillery salutes and a grand ball at the old *palacio*. The subsequent transition from Spanish monarchical to Mexican Republican rule further weakened the structure of government. Economically, the transfer of sovereignty resulted in the opening of the famous Santa Fe Trail. The social impact of Mexican independence was most violently felt in the organization of the Church. Beginning in 1817, politically-minded visitors brought the Franciscans into disfavor, and when Mexico broke with Spain in 1821 all Spanish citizens who would not subscribe to the new regime were ordered from the country. The Franciscans, who were ministering to twenty Indian pueblos and one hundred and two towns and ranches were only slightly affected, the last of the old band remaining until about 1840. The secular clergy from Mexico gradually took over the missions and parishes when the Mexican hierarchy was not prepared to train enough priests for its own spiritual administration. "As for the Mexican Republic expelling Spanish-born clergy who would not subscribe to the new nation," writes Fr. Angélico Chávez,[2] "it did do great harm in Mexico, but in New Mexico the remaining friars were Creoles who did subscribe to the new civil order. Bishop Zubiría then worked hard to establish a native clergy, and he succeeded admirably." The statement of Fr. Theodosius Meyer, O.F.M., who wrote that the regime of the secular clergy from Mexico "cannot very well be written in illuminated letters," is typical of too many writers who have maligned the Mexican secular clergy, apparently in an effort to flatter the English-speaking and French clergy who followed them. The Mexican clergy performed admirably under very trying circumstances.

Even the black sheep of New Mexican church history, Fathers Martínez of Taos and Gallegos of Albuquerque, were not so bad as they are painted, even by Catholic posterity, and these were only two of a trojan, faithful, and zealous band, some of whom, notably Fathers Escolástico Herrera of Santa Clara and Jesús de Baca of Isleta, were of saintly character.

Episcopal visitations were rare in New Mexico during Spanish-Colonial and Mexican Republican times. Previous to the arrival of Father Lamy in 1851, the last episcopal visit had been that of Bishop José Antonio de Zubiría in 1850, he having made a previous visit in 1833. However, ecclesiastical visitators from the Episcopal See at Durango were more frequent. The first visitator to Chimayó, for example, was Fr. Juan Bautista Ladrón de Guevara on May 8, 1818. The second visitation was made on August 29, 1826, by Fr. Agustín Fernández de San Vicente. This visitation is of considerable interest to us. In the records of the church at Santa Cruz, Fr. Fernández is quoted as follows:

> I command you [the parishioners of the Santuario de Chimayó] to remove from the chapel all the *santos* painted on the hides of animals (sobre pieles de animales) and on rough boards (tablas defectuosas) . . .[3]

The visitator states that this order found its origin in a pastoral letter issued to him by the Bishop of Durango, Dr. Juan Bautista de Castañiza. This may be the order referred to by Bourke in 1881, upon the occasion of his purchase of a painting on buffalo hide at Pojoaque:

> . . . about a century ago one of their archbishops directed that all pictures of that class [paintings on animal skin] should be replaced with more pretentious works upon muslin or canvas.[4]

---

2. Personal correspondence.
3. *Bulletin* (mimeographed) of Holy Cross Parish, Santa Cruz, N. M., Aug. 31, 1952.
4. Bloom, "Bourke on the Southwest," *New Mexico Historical Review*, XI, 3 (July, 1936), 247.

Again, it may be that Bourke's informant may have been recalling a tradition of Fr. Domínguez' criticism of 1776. In any case, Bishop Castañiza's pastoral letter did not affect the position of the *bultos* and *retablos* at Chimayó, Santa Cruz, or any other rural New Mexican chapel.

In 1832, one Antonio Barreiro painted a picture of the spiritual administration of New Mexico in words so impassioned that they give the impression of being entirely true. Among other observations of a more than reproachful character he wrote that "there are considerable numbers of unfortunate people who go most Sundays of the year without hearing Mass; the churches are almost in ruins; and most of them are certainly not worthy of being called temples of God."[5] One could interpret the criticism of Barreiro as a reflection on the personal lives and the neglect of the New Mexican clergy. The conditions outlined by him were not the result of neglect, but of the scarcity of clergy, which he himself mentions. "The secular clergy sent up by the Bishop of Durango, not having the missionary vocation, did not stay long upon discovering that the region was still primitive in everything. The few remaining friars," continues Fray Angélico, "old and sickly, had to take over the parishes again. Other clergy came from Durango and stayed, but the work was too much for these few as the last of the Franciscans had died."

It was under these disheartening conditions that the making of sacred images by the villagers and ranchers of northern New Mexico attained the summit of its golden age. This is not only the *santero's* greatest hour, but also that of the religious spirit of the New Mexican people who would not live without his handiwork.

During the 1820's and '30's a large number of English-speaking Americans and French Canadians settled permanently in New Mexico, contemporaneous with the early activities of the Santa Fe traders. The workmanship of the craftsmen among them doubtlessly influenced the New Mexican tradesmen with whom they came in contact. Considering that these were the best days of *santo*-making, it may be that the *americano* had something to do with the art after all.

The first written notice of *santos* by a citizen of the United States was taken by one George Wilkins Kendall, who, with a small group of Americans, during the last days of September and the first days of October, 1841, was in the village of San Miguel del Bado, in the western part of present-day San Miguel County, as a prisoner of the New Mexican governor. News reached the village that a large body of Texans were on their way to capture New Mexico. Kendall describes the consternation of the villagers:

> The wax figure of the patron saint of the place, San Miguel, . . . was dragged from his niche in the little church, mounted upon a large platform, and carried about in procession. A more comical figure than this same San Miguel is would be difficult either to imagine or discover. I cannot say that his saintship had ever been tarred, but he had certainly been feathered from head to foot. From his shoulders hung listlessly a pair of huge, ill-constructed wings, while his head to complete the ludicrous *tout ensemble,* was covered with a lace cap of the fashion of our grandmothers. Another figure, intended to represent the Virgin but nothing more than a doll of the largest size, was carried upon the same platform. . . . Nothing could be more grotesque and laughable than this comical head of St. Michael, . . . whenever this counterfeit presentment of the saint was brought fairly in sight, we lost our gravity entirely, and were compelled to turn aside to conceal our laughter.[6]

Several of the English-speaking Americans who were settled in New Mexico when General Kearny entered Santa Fe in 1846 were directly concerned with the plans and operations which preceded the occupation. The New Mexicans put up little resistance to the American troops, for they had little reason to be either loyal to or affectionate towards the governments of either Spain or Mexico after

5. *Ojeada sobre Nuevo Mexico,* p. 39.
6. *Narrative of the Texan Santa Fe Expedition, 1841,* I, 339–40.

154 years of isolation and neglect. There was much discontent among the New Mexicans with regard to the performance of the Mexican authorities. In 1827, for example, when Governor Pérez imposed direct taxes on the people, a revolution broke out which resulted in the death of the Governor.

In the wake of occupation the migration of Americans assumed the proportions of a flood, not only of human beings but also of material objects and of ideas. The Santa Fe traders extended their activities, and newcomers established themselves in every office and occupation, both public and private. It was not long, however, before New Mexicans fitted out regular caravans and controlled a large portion of the Trail trade. Over the new avenues of commerce new products were introduced which constituted the death knell of the few remaining and long poverty-stricken industries.

The influx of United States citizens resulted in many occasions for mutual misunderstanding. The Americans, for the most part representatives of an English-Protestant civilization, had few kind words for the people of the newly acquired territory, the latter being the underprivileged representatives of a Latin-Roman Catholic civilization. This explains the almost complete absence of sympathy on the part of men like Josiah Gregg, the author of what has been called "the classic of all narratives of the Santa Fe Trail," for anything New Mexican, particularly the religious practices of the people. The fact is that there was no part of their personal background or racial tradition which would help them understand the ways of the New Mexicans, and for this reason they should not be castigated for their sometimes caustic phrases. A few quotations from Gregg will suffice to demonstrate this point:

> The New Mexican appears to have inherited much of the cruelty and intolerance of their ancestors, and no small portion of their bigotry and fanaticism.[7]

> . . . the apparition [Our Lady of Guadalupe] having been canonized by the Pope . . .[8]

> . . . canonized fiestas.[9]

> . . . encouraging the people to bow down and worship this graven image instead of their maker.[10]

> I sincerely hope the bishop will cause such public display of saints and images to be discontinued . . .[11]

Sometime during the last days of March or the first days of April, 1846, Lewis H. Garrard, a seventeen-year-old boy from Cincinnati, reached the village of Taos, and was invited into the home of Céran St. Vrain, a French Canadian who had settled there in 1826 and with whom Garrard had made the trip to New Mexico from Westport, Missouri. Garrard wrote:

> I was ushered into an oblong, handsomely furnished room, with . . . the walls hung with portraits of holy characters, crosses, etc., showing the prevailing religion . . .[12]

On August 30, 1846, Lt. W. H. Emory visited the San Miguel Chapel in Santa Fe:

> The church was crowded with an impressive number of men and women, but not a word was uttered from the pulpit by the priest, who kept his back to the congregation the whole time, repeating prayers and incantations. . . . The interior of the church was decorated with some fifty crosses, a great number of the most miserable paintings, and wax figures and looking-glasses, trimmed with pieces of tinsel.[13]

On the fourth of the following month, Emory stopped at a home in Bernalillo:

> We were led into an oblong room. . . . The walls are hung with miserable pictures of the saints, crosses innumerable, and Yankee mirrors without number.[14]

While in Santa Fe on September 20, 1846, Susan Shelby Magoffin, the wife of Samuel

7. *Commerce of the Prairies,* p. 143.
8. *Ibid.,* p. 165.
9. *Ibid.,* p. 169.
10. *Ibid.,* p. 263.
11. *Ibid.,* p. 247.
12. *Wah-to-Yah and the Taos Trail,* p. 234.
13. *Notes on a Military Reconnoissance* . . . . p. 34.
14. *Ibid.,* p. 39.

Magoffin, a Santa Fe trader in partnership with his more famous brother Santiago, made the following entry in her diary:

> I accompanied the general [Kearny] to church today with the view of seeing the church. . . . There are some defaced pictures hanging about the Altar, the designs of which, for the numberless scratches and fingerprints, I could not unravel. There is also a statue of Christ covered with a net to protect it from injury—near it is a large waxen doll dressed as a priest [!] and is bearing a cross.[15]

Capt. A. R. Johnson visited Albuquerque on September 29, 1846: ". . . the houses being hung with looking-glasses and images."[16]

In 1853 Baldwin Möllhausen accompanied the Whipple expedition across New Mexico in the capacity of topographical draughtsman and naturalist. The interior of the church at Santo Domingo was the only one described by him:

> . . . the walls were of smooth clay, on which hung some old Spanish pictures,—the sole decoration, with the exception of some rude Indian paintings, among which we remarked the figure of a man on horseback riding over a troop of men: a *Conquestador* [sic], therefore, and evidently an allusion to the Spanish conquest. The Catholic and Aztec religions were evidently blended in these representations; the Holy Virgin is often found in company with an Indian figure denominated Montezuma . . .[17]

As the image of St. James the Greater conquering the Saracen hosts is limited to Hispanic art, Möllhausen may be forgiven for his failure to recognize it. It would not be hazarding a guess to say that the "Indian figure denominated Montezuma" was none other than good old St. Joseph.

Lt. A. W. Whipple describes the same painting:

> The most curious object noticed was an ox-skin banner, apparently very old, and painted to represent, in profile, a singular figure; with buckler and shield, a visor, lance, and sword, complete; all riding at full speed over prostrate warriors, whose upturned faces expressed great consternation.[18]

W. W. H. Davis, a Pennsylvania judge, was in Santa Fe in 1856: "The family room is adorned with a number of rude engravings of saints, among which the Virgin of Guadalupe is always conspicuous."[19]

Later he wrote:

> They [the New Mexicans] have an abiding faith in saints and images, and with the mass of the inhabitants their worship appears no more than a blind adoration of these insensible objects. Some of the most intelligent of the better class look upon these bits of wood as all-powerful in every emergency; and upon the occasion of a fire in Santa Fe a few years ago, a prominent Mexican gentleman was anxious that one of the wooden saints should be brought from the church to quench the flames. . . . Upon one occasion, when visiting a family, a member of which was quite ill, a number of friends came in with a small image of a favorite saint. . . I left them in the midst of their semi-heathen incantations. . . . The sick person recovered, and I have no doubt another miraculous cure was placed to the credit of the dingy little image.[20]

After viewing a Good Friday procession in Santa Fe, Davis stated:

> The image of the Savior, and others of a similar character that held a prominent place in the exercises, were disgusting to the sight, and failed to create in my mind other feelings than those of pity for the worshipers of these unmeaning bits of ill-carved wood.[21]

The American occupation of New Mexico was quickly followed by Church action. On July 19, 1850, Pope Pius IX made New Mexico a vicariate apostolic, and on the twenty-third of the same month appointed the Rev. John B. Lamy, from the diocese of Cincinnati, as vicar apostolic. Father Lamy arrived in Santa Fe on August 8, 1851, and was received

---

15. *Down the Santa Fe Trail* . . . , pp. 137–38.
16. Emory, *op. cit.,* p. 568.
17. *Diary of a Journey from the Mississippi to the Coasts of the Pacific,* I, 336–37.
18. *Reports of Exploration and Surveys for a Railway Route,* III, 46.
19. *El Gringo or New Mexico and Her People,* p. 180.
20. *Ibid.,* pp. 225–26.
21. *Ibid.,* p. 346.

with enthusiasm by the people in general, although a few of the clergy and some of the well-to-do caused him a deal of embarrassment and trouble.

Father Joseph P. Macheboeuf, who accompanied Father Lamy to New Mexico, gave the following description of the new vicar's reception in Santa Fe:

> . . . the entry of Bishop Lamy into the Capitol was truly a triumphant one. The Governor of the Territory with all the civil and military authorities, and thousands of people, met him six miles out from the city with the finest carriages and coaches of the city. . . .
>
> As the monster procession neared the city the commander of the fort ordered a salute of artillery in the Bishop's honor, and the glad shouts of the people met him at every turn. . . .[22]

It has often been written that Father Lamy's disapproval of New Mexican *santos* was so marked that he ordered them removed from the chapels and churches of the territory and that they be replaced with conventional plaster images, prints, and paintings on canvas. Considering his European background, it may be assumed that he did not find this folk art entirely to his aesthetic taste. There is no question but that the newly arrived American clergy, mostly men of northern European origin, desired better church ornaments and furniture, for in some of the larger towns houses of worship were soon stripped of their old images. James F. Meline, after quoting Emory's description of the San Miguel Chapel, stated:

> This statement, I make no doubt, was perfectly correct in 1846, but things have greatly changed, for two Sundays ago (just twenty years later) I attended service there, and of wax figures and tinsel and looking-glasses, there was no sign. I do not see any particular harm, except as a matter of taste, in fifty crosses. Nevertheless, there are not but one or two in the church.[23]

San Felipe de Neri in Albuquerque was completely changed over:

> This church—above other Mexican churches —is quite aristocratic in having a board floor.

Some half-dozen long kneeling benches used for pews at the upper end, show the extent of American innovation.[24]

Santa Gertrudis at Mora was replaced, building and all: "We went to the church, which appears to be a modern adobe building, neat and clean interior, little or no ornament, dirt floor."[25]

There is a tradition in and around Santa Fe that the people of the capital hid their *santos* during the first years of the new vicar's residence among them. The removal of the old *retablos* and *bultos* from the San Miguel Chapel could easily have alarmed them. The fact that they were removed shows that Father Lamy thought them undesirable, but he soon must have made another estimate of their meaning, for we know from Davis' observation in 1856, only five years after Lamy's arrival, that *santos* were carried in the Good Friday procession in Santa Fe, a ceremony in which the new vicar himself participated.

The conclusion reached is that Lamy never wrote an order for the removal of folk art from the chapels and churches, that he probably expressed his disapproval of them orally, and that he later experienced a change in attitude. Furthermore, his oral expression seems never to have carried into the Upper Rio Grande Valley, for the chapels and churches of this area have never been without folk-made religious paintings and statuary since the beginnings of this art.

One of the issues of what has been called "the secular interlude" of New Mexican history, 1797–1850, is the society called *La Sociedad* (or *Hermandad*) *de Nuestro Padre Jesús,* sometimes with *Nazareno* added, and some of the post-Lamy groups calling themselves *Los Hermanos Penitentes de la Tercera Orden de San Francisco.* This is a religious brotherhood of laymen who still practice flagellation in some rural sections of New Mexico and southern Colorado. Bishop Lamy

22. Howlett, *Life of the Right Reverend Joseph P. Machebeuf, D.D.*, pp. 165–66.

23. *Two Thousand Miles on Horseback*, p. 190.

24. *Ibid.*, p. 125.

25. *Ibid.*, p. 110.

and his successor Salpointe were in the dark concerning the origin of the *Penitentes*. The history of flagellants began in several places during the Middle Ages, in Italy in 1260 and in Germany and northwest Europe in 1348, where they were organized into heretical sects. Flagellation was introduced early into Spain, where it still persists to a minor degree. In New Mexico it is neither a link in the chain of European and New World history of flagellants nor an offshoot of the Third Order of St. Francis, as stated over and over again by both journalists and scholars of serious bent. The founder of New Mexico, Juan de Oñate, and his companions flagellated themselves during Holy Week of 1598 upon the occasion of their entry, which has led subsequent writers to date the beginnings of the society with the genesis of the New Mexican colony. The fact is that the *Penitentes* were not known to exist as late as 1776, and are first mentioned in 1833. This has led Fr. Angélico Chávez to set upon the years between 1790 and 1810 as those which witnessed the origin of the society in New Mexico. He further concludes that the immediate inspiration of the New Mexican groups were the confraternities of Seville, Spain, whose practices they closely resemble, and that the society took root in New Mexico because of one single factor, "the spirit of primitive Christian penance inherent in the Spanish soul for centuries after it disappeared from Christendom in general."[26]

In 1849, two years before Lamy arrived in Santa Fe, and at a time when the Mexican and New Mexican secular clergy were struggling against almost impossible odds due mainly to the scarcity of priests, the first ministers of Protestant denominations appeared in the territory, and before long had a number of missions in various sections of the Upper and Lower Rio Grande valleys and in southern Colorado. They went so far as to organize *Penitente* groups that had been reprimanded by the Catholic clergy into Protestant sects, thus making life that much more uncomfortable for the already harassed Catholic pastors. The poor old *santos* received their

share of ridicule from these well-meaning gentlemen.[27]

As the century wore on, government representatives continued to arrive in New Mexico on one mission or another. Of those accounts written during the last quarter of the nineteenth century, that of Lt. John Gregory Bourke is of the most pertinence to this study. On July 15, 1881, Bourke visited the church at Pojoaque:

> . . . bought an old oil painting, taken from the old ruined church of Pojuaque or Nambe, I couldn't learn which, but have reason to think the latter. It is a representation on raw Buffalo hide, and in crude style of Santiago, mounted upon a prancing white charger, and carrying in his right hand a lance, from which floats a pennant inscribed with a cross, the same emblem being displayed upon the shield he bears in his left hand. The Saint is emerging from the clouds above the chivalry of Spain who, with renewed courage, are pressing upon the foe, whose bodies strew the ground in heaps. The design, so far as may be discerned through the ravages of time, is crude and unfinished with, however, a few faint traces of artistic skill and power. The account the Indians gave of it is that it was formerly the altarpiece of one of their churches, Nambe, I think, and that about a century ago one of their archbishops directed that all pictures of that class (Buffalo Hide) should be replaced with more pretentious works upon muslin or canvas. This decree banished to the retirement of a private house, the effort upon which some pious priest had probably concentrated all his artistic skill for weeks, or perhaps months.[28]

The same day he visited Pojoaque, Bourke examined the church at Santa Cruz:

> Within . . . there is a niche containing [a] life-sized statue of Our Savior, Blessed Virgin, and one or two Saints, all of them, as might be expected, barbarous in execution.
>
> Facing this niche is a larger wall painting, divided into panels, each devoted to some conven-

26. *See* Chávez, "The Penitentes of New Mexico," *New Mexico Historical Review*, XXIX, 2 (April, 1954), 97–123.
27. *See* Craig, *Our Mexicans, passim.*
28. Bloom, *op. cit.*, p. xi, 247.

tional Roman Catholic picture, which, in spite of the ignorance of the artist, could be recognized.[29]

On the nineteenth of the same month he was at the Church of San José de Gracia at Las Trampas:

> The paintings were on wood and were I disposed to be sarcastic I would remark that they ought to be burned up with the hideous dolls of saints to be seen in one of the niches in the transept.[30]

Remarking on the images in the church at Pojoaque, which he revisited on July 23, Bourke wrote:

> Upon the walls are numerous paintings of saints, some of which manifest an improvement in artistic taste and skill over those I've seen elsewhere. There are several which, if properly cleaned, would be, I think, very beautiful, notably that of Our Lady of Guadalupe, over the main altar.[31]

The *Guadalupe* mentioned is not a folk representation, but an oil on canvas now in the Museum of New Mexico. It was rescued from the church by a Pojoaque family before the edifice was razed in 1922.

"Near the altar," Bourke continues, "is a crucifix whereon hangs Our Savior, his body raw with crimson wounds, and in attendance upon him a decidedly dumpy little angel."[32]

Bourke also testified to the extensive ownership of New Mexican *santos* by the Pueblo Indians, mentioning the presence of many *bultos* and other images and crosses at San Juan, Santa Ana, Zía and Jémez.

At Zía on November 5:

> The wooden figure of the Savior on the Cross must have been intended to convey to the minds of the simple natives the idea that our Lord had been butchered by the Apaches. If so, the artist has done his work well.[33]

At Jémez on November 5:

> The idols were duplicates of those secured last night from the house where, cheek by jowl, they vied in hideousness with the tin-framed,

painted and begrimed daubs of San Antonio, San Juan and San Diego.[34]

Bourke was followed into New Mexico by one Ernest Ingersoll, who in the summer of 1885 was in Ojo Caliente, a village in the southwestern bulge of Taos County:

> Opposite the hotel and springs was a poor little Mexican hamlet called also Ojo Caliente, where an odd church invited inspection.[35]
>
> On either side of the altar, facing each other, hung crosses bearing wooden figures of Christ crucified. . . . These effigies were painted a dull white, and hung in the most agonizing attitudes, —suffering intensified by the long-drawn lines of the haggard faces, the slant of the eyes, and the drooping of the lower jaw. To produce a more horrible representation still, the carver had given the forms extreme emaciation, the ribs standing apart, the abdomen sunken, the bones and cords of all the limbs dreadfully prominent. Add to this cadaverous appearance a network of red streaks tracing the principle veins, and great splashes and runlets of blood, and you have an image awful beyond conception . . .; and in several niches, small, tinsel-clothed puppets, which the man told me were San Francisco, Patron of the Church, and Our Lady of Guadalupe. . . . The little church is not to be despised, and the awe-struck faith of its miracle-loving parishioners may be more acceptable than the gilded worship of many a rich and learned congregation nearer the sea.[36]

The folk art of religious image-making was dying by the time Ingersoll came to New Mexico, and after his observations a period of forty years was to elapse before *santos* were again to attract the interest of a written commentary.[37]

It is disappointing, but not surprising, that neither Sister Blandina Segale (1872–92),

29. Bourke, *Field notes* . . . , pp. 44, 1577.
30. *Ibid.*, pp. 44, 1635.
31. *Ibid.*, pp. 45, 1717.
32. *Ibid.*, pp. 45, 1717–18.
33. Bloom, *op. cit.*, p. xi, 222.
34. *Ibid.*, xi, 233.
35. *The Crest of the Continent*, p. 87.
36. *Ibid.*, pp. 90–91.
37. Mabel Dodge Luhan, "The Santos of New Mexico," *The Arts*, March, 1925.

Father Defouri (1887), Bishop Salpointe (1898), nor Father Howlett (1906) took the slightest notice in their writings of the widespread presence of *santos* during their active years in New Mexico and Colorado. Of the six general historians of New Mexico, Prince (1883), Ritch (1883), Bancroft (1889), Twitchell (1911), Read (1912), and Bloom (1933) only Prince makes any mention of New Mexican folk art, and he only in the form of a valueless comparison of an image of St. Joseph by a *santero* with a sophisticated representation of Our Lady then in the church of Our Lady of Guadalupe in Santa Fe.

The population of the young and growing United States was not noted for its art discernment, especially the pioneers of the West. Therefore, it is not too surprising that in the early days of American occupation the old weatherbeaten adobe chapels and rough-hewn and simply drawn religious folk simulacra of New Mexico did not attract the interest, much less arouse the enthusiasm, of either political or social historians or church authorities. Today the old home-made sacred images of New Mexico have achieved a new recognition, what with being the object of serious study and of collection by individuals and institutions, and of exhibition in many of the nation's important museums. For this we may

thank a handful of discerning and cultured *americanos*.

Perhaps no one has been more deeply and sincerely affected by the handiwork of the old *santeros* than an architect and an historian of our own day, who have fashioned in beauty and understanding the jewel of all expressions on the religious folk craftsmanship of New Mexico:

> One can imagine the emotions of St. Francis if he could come back to earth and look over the thousands of churches that have been built in his name throughout the world—cathedrals made magnificent with the gold of the Americas; diminutive chapels enriched only with the devotion of simple souls to whom Life and the Faith are one. It is a safe guess that on no others in this wide world would his gaze rest with such deep affection as upon the poor sanctuaries of New Mexico, most of them built of the very earth on which they stand by the labor of unpaid worshippers; embellished only with such decorations as could be carved with crude hand-made tools and earthen colors from the native soil. These little plazas display the poverty that was to him the first essential of holiness. These simple people are like the peasant folk of his beloved Assisi—like the "common people" who listened gladly to the "Wayfarer in Galilee."[38]

38. Hewett and Fisher, *Mission Monuments of New Mexico*, p. 120.

plates

NEW MEXICAN SACRED ART OF MEXICAN ORIGIN

1. *Nuestra Señora del Carmen,* Our Lady of Mt. Carmel. Height: 3'4". Church of the Holy Cross, Santa Cruz, New Mexico.
2. *El Santo Niño de Atocha,* The Christ Child of Atocha. Lithograph. Cady Wells Collection, Museum of New Mexico.
3. *Nuestra Señora del Pueblecito,* Our Lady of the Village. Steel engraving. Museum of New Mexico. Photograph by Ernest Knee.
4. *Nuestra Señora la Reina de los Cielos,* Our Lady Queen of Heaven. Oil on copper. 7" × 9". Author's collection.
5. *San Juan Nepomuceno, Mártir,* St. John Nepomucene, Martyr. Oil on linen. 11½" × 15⅝". Gilberto Espinosa Collection.
6. *Nuestra Señora de Begoña,* Our Lady of Begoña. Tempera on elkskin. 42" × 56". Church of Santa Cruz, Galisteo, New Mexico.
7. *San José y el Santo Niño,* St. Joseph and the Christ Child. Tempera on elkskin. 56" × 68". Church of San José, Laguna Pueblo, New Mexico. Photograph by Lee H. Harmon.
8. *San Jerónimo, Doctor y Conf.,* St. Jerome, Doctor and Conf. Fragment. Tempera on wood. *ca.* 1700. 10" × 22". Harwood Foundation Collection, Taos.

NEW MEXICAN RELIGIOUS FOLK ART

EARLY COPYING

9. *San José, Patriarca y Conf.,* St. Joseph, Patriarch and Conf. Height: 18½". Gilberto Espinosa Collection.
10. *San Miguel Arcángel,* St. Michael the Archangel. Fragment. 11¾" × 24⅜". Museum of New Mexico.

RETABLOS

Single Panels and Altar-Screens

11. Altar-Screen, Church of San José, Laguna Pueblo, New Mexico. By the Laguna Painter. 14' × 13'7½". Top panel: The Most Holy Trinity. Lower section, left to right: St. John Nepomucene, Priest and Martyr. St. Joseph and the Christ Child. St. Barbara, Virgin and Martyr. Photograph by Lee H. Harmon, before restoration in 1950.
12. *Cristo Crucificado.* By the Calligraphic Painter. 8⅔" × 12½". Harwood Foundation Collection, Taos.
13. *El Divino Rostro,* Veronica's Veil. By the Calligraphic Painter. On tabernacle door. 11⅗" × 31¼". Cady Wells Collection, Museum of New Mexico.
14. *San Miguel Arcángel,* St. Michael the Archangel. By the Chili Painter. 14½" × 22¼". Harwood Foundation Collection, Taos.

15. *Cristo Cargado de la Cruz,* Christ Carrying His Cross. By the Chili Painter. 10¹⁵⁄₁₆″ × 15⁷⁄₁₆″. Norma Fiske Day Collection, Museum of New Mexico.

16. *Nuestra Señora del Carmen,* Our Lady of Mt. Carmel. By El Niño Perdido Painter. 10⅖″ × 11¼″. Norma Fiske Day Collection, Museum of New Mexico.

17. *Nuestra Señora de San Juan de los Lagos,* Our Lady of San Juan de los Lagos. By José Aragón. 6¼″ × 8¹⁵⁄₁₆″. Cady Wells Collection, Museum of New Mexico.

18. *Nuestra Señora la Reina de los Cielos,* Our Lady Queen of Heaven. By José Rafael Aragón. 10″ × 8¼″. Harwood Foundation Collection, Taos.

19. *San Cayetano, Conf.,* St. Cajetan, Conf. By José Rafael Aragón. 8″ × 10½″. Herbert I. Spinden Collection.

20. *El Sumo Sacerdote Melquisedec,* The High Priest Melchisedech. *San Miguel Arcángel,* St. Michael the Archangel. *Moisés, Profeta,* Moses, Prophet. By Miguel Aragón. 12½″ × 15¾″. New Mexico Historical Society, Museum of New Mexico.

21. Altar-Screen from the Durán Chapel near Talpa, New Mexico. By José Rafael Aragón. 7′7½″ × 9′7″. Upper left: *Nuestra Señora de los Dolores,* Our Lady of Sorrows. Lower left: *Same subject.* Upper center: *La Santísima Trinidad,* The Most Holy Trinity. Lower center: *Nuestro Padre Jesús,* The Man of Sorrows. Upper right: *San Francisco de Asís,* St. Francis of Assisi. Lower right: *Nuestra Señora de la Soledad,* Our Lady of Solitude. Photograph courtesy of the Detroit Institute of Arts.

22. *Nuestra Señora de los Dolores,* Our Lady of Sorrows. By Miguel Aragón. 7¼″ × 13¹⁄₃″. Harwood Foundation Collection, Taos.

23. *San Ignacio de Loyola, Conf.,* St. Ignatius Loyola, Conf. By a Fourth Aragón.

7⅜″ × 11⅝″. Norma Fiske Day Collection, Museum of New Mexico.

24. *Pietá.* By the Oriental Painter. 17″ × 14″. Cady Wells Collection, Museum of New Mexico.

25. *San Ignacio de Loyola, Conf.,* St. Ignatius Loyola, Conf. By the Dot-Dash Painter. 16″ × 20½″ on right, 20¼″ on left. Cady Wells Collection, Museum of New Mexico.

26. *San Ramón Nonato,* Conf., St. Raymond Nonnatus, Conf. By the Dot-Dash Painter. 6½″ × 10½″. Harwood Foundation Collection, Taos.

27. *La Santísima Trinidad,* The Most Holy Trinity. By the Quill Pen Painter. 12¹⁄₁₆″ × 12¾″. Norma Fiske Day Collection, Museum of New Mexico.

28. *Nuestra Señora del Rosario,* Our Lady of the Rosary. By the Quill Pen Painter. With shell: 12¾ × 22⅔″. Cady Wells Collection, Museum of New Mexico.

29. *San Acacio del Monte Ararat, Mártir,* St. Acacius of Mt. Ararat, Martyr. By the Floral Painter. 11³⁄₁₆″ × 12⅝″. Cady Wells Collection, Museum of New Mexico.

30. The Hispanic Society of America Panels, New York. Center panel: Christ Crucified (A). 28½″ × 13¹⁄₇″. Top row, left to right: Our Lady of Sorrows (D). 11⅖″ × 6⅘″. Our Lady of Mt. Carmel (A). 14¹⁄₆″ × 7⁹⁄₁₀″. St. Anthony of Padua (B). 11⅔″ × 7¼″. Second row, left to right: St. Cajetan (A). 7⅖″ × 3¹⁄₃″. Christ Crucified (D). 8⅗″ × 6⅘″. Third row, left to right: St. Joseph and the Christ Child (C). 10⅘″ × 7⅔″. Our Lady of Solitude (D). 10¼″ × 6⅗″. Bottom row, left to right: Our Lady of Guadalupe (C). 12⅗″ × 8¼″. St. Anthony of Padua (C). 14¾″ × 8⅔″. Photograph courtesy of the Hispanic Society of America. A—By the Calligraphic Painter. B—By José Rafael Aragón. C—By the Chili Painter. D—Unidentified painter.

BULTOS

Figures in the Round

31. *San Jerónimo, Doctor y Conf.,* St. Jerome, Doctor and Conf. Santa Cruz
Valley Group. Height: 16½". The Taylor Museum.

32. *El Santo Entierro,* Christ in the Sep-
ulcher. Santa Cruz Valley Group.
Corpus: 5'11". Church of the Holy
Cross, Santa Cruz, New Mexico.

33. *Nuestra Señora de Guadalupe,* Our Lady
of Guadalupe. Santa Cruz Valley Group.
Height: 29¾". New Mexico Historical
Society, Museum of New Mexico.

34. *San Ramón Nonato, Conf.,* St. Raymond
Nonnatus, Conf. Santa Cruz Valley
Group. Height: 19½". The Taylor
Museum.

35. *Jesús Nazareno,* The Man of Sorrows.
Taos Group. Height: 28½". Gilberto
Espinosa Collection.

36. *Jesús es Cargado con la Cruz,* Christ
Carrying His Cross. Taos Group.
Height: 28". Note badly reconstructed
arm. This image has the appearance of
having been a representation of St.
Joseph. Harwood Foundation Collection, Taos.

37. *San José, Patriarca y Conf.,* St. Joseph,
Patriarch and Confessor. Arroyo Hondo
Group. Height: 34¾". Cady Wells Col-
lection, Museum of New Mexico.

38. *San Buenaventura, Doctor y Conf.,* St.
Bonaventure, Doctor and Conf. Arroyo
Hondo Group. Height: 28". The Taylor
Museum.

39. *San Rafael Arcángel,* St. Raphael the
Archangel. Tomé Area Group. Height:
24½". Spanish Colonial Arts Society
Collection, Museum of New Mexico.

40. *Cristo Crucificado.* From Valencia, New
Mexico. Height: 3'9½". Church of
Cristo Rey, Santa Fe, New Mexico.

41. *San Isidro Labrador, Conf.,* St. Isidore
the Husbandman, Conf. Mora Group.
Height: 27½". Mrs. Adele Wright Collection, Antelope Ranch, Roll, Arizona.

42. *Cristo Crucificado.* Gothic Group.
Height: 31½". Gilberto Espinosa Collection.

43. *Cristo Crucificado.* Gothic Group.
Height: 18". Cady Wells Collection.
Museum of New Mexico.

44. *Cristo Crucificado.* By Antonio Silva of
Adelino and Tomé. Height: 5'7".
Church of La Inmaculada Concepción,
Tomé, New Mexico.

45. *San Isidro Labrador, Conf.,* St. Isidore
the Husbandman. Probably by Eusebio
Córdova of Córdova. Height. 21¼".
Cady Wells Collection, Museum of New
Mexico.

46. *Cristo Crucificado.* By Juan Ramón Ve-
lásquez of Canjilón. Height: 42½".
McCormick Collection, Museum of New
Mexico.

Unless otherwise indicated, all photographs are the work of the author.

1

Sto NIÑO DE ATOCHA

2

3

4

5

6

7

8

9

10

11

12

13

14

15

16

17

18

19

20

21

22

23

24

25

26

27

28

29

30

31

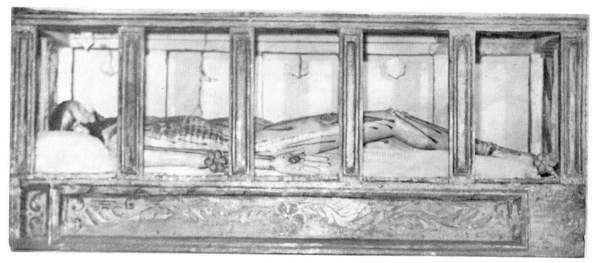

32

33

34

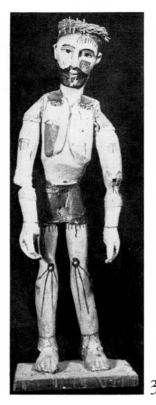

35

36

37

38

39

40

41

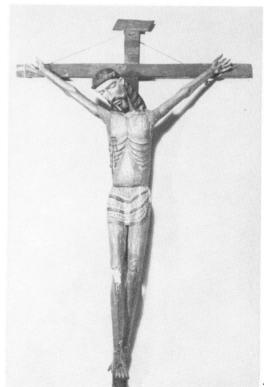

42

43

44

45

46

5. the classification & technology of santos

A. CLASSIFICATION

NEW MEXICAN religious folk images may be considered under three major classifications:

1. *Retablos:* Paintings on *yeso*-coated pine panels in tempera.
2. *Bultos*: Various types of figures carved in the round out of cottonwood (rarely pine), coated with *yeso*, and painted in tempera.
3. Paintings on animal skins in tempera.

1. RETABLOS

A *retablo*, sometimes called a *tabla* (board), is a painting in tempera colors on a slab or panel of pine previously coated with one or more layers of *yeso* (gesso). A group of these panels, forming what is known in English as an altar-piece, altar-screen, retable, or reredos, is also called a *retablo*. Before American occupation the panels or boards used for making *retablos* were hand-adzed; after this time milled boards were used in a great number of cases. *Retablos* are in every size, from a few inches square to 18″ × 20″, the most common dimensions being around 8″ × 10″. There is a unique example in the Kleijkamp and Monroe Collection of a tiny *retablo* of *El Niño Perdido,* The Lost Christ Child, held by a *bulto* representing the same advocation, which measures 1¾″ × 2½″. There are a few exceptionally large *retablos*, such as the representations of *San José, Nuestra Señora del Carmen* and *San Pedro* of the Taylor Museum, which measure 40″ × 30″, 43½″ × 28½″, and 43″ × 33″, respective-ly. Again there are the still larger *retablos* which go to make up the different panels of altar-screens.

There are two types of *retablos*:

Type 1. A Flat Painting. A multiplicity of border treatments and stylistic differences are the only features which distinguish these flat paintings from each other. Some are without any frame whatever, and others have a simulated frame painted along the borders. Some of these painted frames are in solid colors while others are highly decorative. Also, there are a very few cases where frames are simulated by laying straw in geometric patterns along the edge. Sometimes a decorative heading is added in the form of a semicircular lunette, or shell, either as part of the main board or as a separate piece attached to it. Other *retablos* have a frame which is carved along the borders, sometimes with a carved heading added. Again, this frame may be made from a separate piece of moulding glued or doweled or both to the panel, either along the edge or away from the edge and separating the image from the decorated border. This variety may also have a decorative heading. Other *retablos* have a simulated, painted frame and a carved and painted heading. One of the most attractive is the round panel framed with a raised border and further decorated with four or more lunettes, such as the image of *San Mateo* in the Taylor Museum.

New Mexican altar-screens, made up of a number of panels, often display superior artistry (Pl. 21), destined as they were for the most prominent positions in the churches and chapels. The stylistic differences between the panels of some reredos show that they were cooperative projects, while others plainly indicate the workmanship of a single artist.

Type 2. Bas-reliefs. This is a painting of an image carved or modeled in bas-relief, the carving and modeling or both being done in *yeso* previously applied to the pine panel. Some *retablos* of this type limit the use of modeling or carving to the features of the person represented, the rest of the image being exclusively brush work. This type is generally the poorest of all New Mexican *santos*, although a bas-relief of Our Lady of Sorrows in the Kleijkamp and Monroe Collection is unusually well done.

Yeso-coated pine crosses with the image of Christ painted thereon are also found in New Mexican folk art, although they are not at all common. A very archaic-looking, but still attractive image of this kind is in the Museum of New Mexico.

2. BULTOS

A *bulto* is an image carved in the round. Cottonwood is the usual material, although pine is sometimes, if rarely, used. It may be in one piece or in parts held together by glue, dowels, muslin, leather strips, or a combination of these. The Spanish word *bulto* means "form" or "body," and implies a solid object. The word has several more specific meanings, such as "bust," "figure," and "image of a person." It is not a New Mexican colloquialism.

New Mexican *bultos* range in height from the tiny one- or two-inch figures of the Christ Child held by the Virgin, St. Joseph, or St. Anthony, to almost life-size, the last mentioned being mostly representations of Christ Crucified or the Man of Sorrows. These are prominent around Tomé, Valencia and Taos.

Avoiding a consideration of minor differences, which would call for endless discussion, New Mexican *bultos* may be classified under seven distinct types:

Type 1. Small statuary. Images not more than eight inches in height, carved *en bloc* in a few cases, but mostly with the arms and head carved separately.

Type 2. A *bulto-retablo*, or an image carved in the round, painted, and then glued or tied to a panel.

The remaining five types are larger images, ranging in size from about eight inches to almost life-size:

Type 3. Made with the head, arms and legs carved separately. Sometimes the upper arm, the forearm, the hands, and even the fingers on very large *bultos* are also made separately. The parts of the leg may also be made separately.

Type 4. Like Type 2, but with the head and torso carved *en bloc*.

Type 5. *Santo de palo*. *Palo*, in this case, means a rough, unfinished block, small log, or branch. The head, and arms and their parts, are made separately. The body is made of a single piece or block of wood, either crudely shaped or left in its original shape. Clothing, in the form of a robe or a dress, covers the unfinished trunk.

Type 6. The head and torso *en bloc*. The arms, head and torso may be separate parts. The body from the hipline down is formed by tightly stretching any kind of cotton cloth over a framework of wooden staves or reeds set into a base. A supporting pine post often connects the torso to the base, which in the case of some Virgins is set into an arc-shaped base.

Type 7. Crucifixes.

a. *Penitente* Crucifixes. The term is exclusively New Mexican and refers to a class which can always be identified by the sanguinary and gaunt character of the representation of Christ on the Cross. It is found principally in the homes, chapels and churches of the Upper Rio Grande Valley and in southern Colorado. The name derives from the fact that it was the class most used in the *morada*, or chapter house, of *los hermanos penitentes*, the lay organization of flagellants.

b. Crucifixes not of *Penitente* Character. This class is generally smaller than the *penitente* kind, are seldom life-size, and do not make an issue of the horrible details of crucifixion.

3. PAINTINGS ON ANIMAL SKINS IN TEMPERA

On page 99 are listed 26 paintings on elk-skin, deerskin, and buffalo hide, all done in Mexico during the seventeenth and eighteenth centuries by artists of considerable skill. Between 1800 and 1850, along with *retablos* and *bultos*, a limited number of paintings in tempera on animal skins were executed by the same folk craftsmen who worked with and on wood.

B. TECHNOLOGY

The technology of *santo*-making involved three distinct sets of operations: 1) the carving and joining of the wood, in the case of *bultos*; 2) the preparation of the wood surface and the application of the *yeso*; and 3) the preparation and application of the tempera colors.

Careful examination of the old *bultos* and *retablos* plainly discloses the techniques and materials employed in most aspects of the first two sets of operations. The question of the materials used in the preparation of pigments and the methods of their preparation and application is, however, one which presents many problems yet to be resolved. Previous to January, 1951, students of New Mexican *santos* were obliged to rely almost exclusively upon a consideration of the economic limitations and the known resources of the areas where *santos* were executed, in their efforts to determine the materials and sources of pigments. In the month and year mentioned, Gettens and Turner published the results of the first scientific inquiry into this matter.[1] Excepting the findings of these scientists, the observations offered herein relating to the sources, the preparation and the application of pigments and colors are deductions made upon the basis of known factors.

1. THE CARVING AND JOINING OF THE WOOD

The most superficial examination of New Mexican folk-made religious images discloses that the *santero* manifested a high degree of ingenuity in their execution, for he utilized even those materials which his stingy environment made every effort to place beyond his reach. He gathered and processed a wide assortment of natural products, both vegetable and animal, wood, of course, being the foundation of his craft. With few exceptions, *bultos* were made of cottonwood, and *retablos* of pine. Cottonwood, which is light brown, is a weak wood, and when seasoned is easier to shape than pine. The latter, a more finely-grained wood, and harder than cottonwood when seasoned, was avoided in the making of *bultos*, undoubtedly because of its resistance to poor tools. For very small *bultos* the root of the cottonwood was especially desirable, since its grain is not disturbed by imperfections.

The *santero* generally used tools of his own or of local manufacture, although it is possible that he possessed some imported implements. Even a cursory examination of *santos* discloses the use of the crudest sort of instruments. This is most visible in the details of small parts, and is also seen on the backs of *retablos* and on the backs and other hidden parts of *bultos*, where efforts to smooth the surface have scarcely disturbed the roughness of hand-adzed cuts, knife cutting and shaping. The surface to be painted, whether on *retablos* or *bultos*, was much better finished, which must have taken a deal of time and patience.

Only smaller *bultos*, not much more than eight inches in height, were ever carved *en bloc*, but even these figures generally have the arms made separately and then joined to the body. In the case of larger figures, where the legs were to be revealed, these, along with the head and arms, were carved individually and then joined to the torso with glue and dowels. Also with larger figures, all parts of the limbs, including the fingers, were sometimes made separately and then joined in the manner described, except that fingers were generally joined only with glue. Nails were never used to hold the various parts of a *bulto* together, as metal in any form was too precious; also,

---

1. "The Materials and Methods of Some Religious Paintings of Early Nineteenth-Century New Mexico," EP, 58, 1 (January, 1951), 3–16.

nails would split the wood too easily. Elbow and shoulder joints, especially on large figures, were commonly made of muslin or other cloth. On figures of Christ this method would effect articulation whenever this was desired. Very often a cloth covering served to hide the lines of union at any part of the figure. Although the heads of large figures were usually carved separately, there are examples showing the head and torso carved *en bloc*.

In Type 6, which is made by tightly stretching and sewing any available kind of cotton cloth over a framework of wooden staves or reeds set into a base, the cotton cloth was covered with several coats of *yeso* and then painted with either floral or other decorative patterns. The staves number from four to eight, and the base is made in proportion to the flare of the skirt on images of the Virgin. This structure, known in English as the "candlestick" method, is also found in representations of Christ and some saints. In Marian representations the head is sometimes in the half-round, the flat back being covered with a *yeso*-coated cloth veil, showing the length to which the old *santeros* went to save time, materials, and effort. Only in the case of very large figures, such as that of *Nuestra Señora de los Dolores* at Manzano, would this method of construction be a time- and work-saver, and considering the size and number of the staves and the size of the supporting post, neither would it serve to reduce the weight of the image. The skirt of the *Señora* at Manzano is unpainted, the intention being to clothe the image.

In the case of the *Corpus* on crucifixes, the various parts of the limbs are generally made separately. Excepting the feet, this is also true of other representations, although there are examples of the feet having been carved separately on figures other than those of Christ Crucified. The line of union of the forearm and the upper arm, in the case of both small and large figures, is often strengthened by running it upward from the front of the elbow joint to the middle-back of the upper arm, or even higher. On Mora figures (*q.v.*; see frontispiece) the upper arms of Christ Cruci-

fied sometimes take in a part of the shoulders and breast, thus offering an even greater area of union for more strength.

On *penitente* crucifixes the wound in the side of Our Lord is of gaping proportions, sometimes hollowed out to hold a liquid container and a wick from which simulated blood dripped into a chalice held by an angel. These images have wigs of red, brown, or black human hair, often are carved to wear crowns of real thorns, and generally are robed in red. As this class was sometimes intended for use in representing the various scenes of the Passion, the head and all the joints were often articulated with muslin or leather, although a peg and socket arrangement at the arm and shoulder joints is not unknown. The *Santo Entierro*, Christ in the Sepulcher, in the Taylor Museum is an amazing example of the use of mechanical devices to produce an illusion of life. Below the left shoulder blade is a deep, oval-shaped opening through which the ribs, made of quills, may be seen. Behind the ribs the suspended heart "palpitates" when the image is moved. A superb example of a large New Mexican crucifix is in the church of Santo Tomás at Abiquiú, which also has a "palpitating" heart. An unusually large crucifix, 7′ 9½″ in height, from the Durán Chapel, Talpa, is installed over the stairway in the Taylor Museum.

The ribs of most New Mexican crucifixes are frequently indicated by incised grooves or by simple incisions, and at other times by simple incisions sanded out into furrows.

It was also common practice to carve the teeth and tongue in *bultos*, particularly of Christ Crucified.

The superscription INRI is found on most New Mexican Crucifixes. Whenever it is missing the peg holes on or the groove along the upper extremity of the perpendicular beam are evidence of the original presence of a superscription. The panel bearing the superscription may be in any number of shapes, from that of various kinds of parallelograms to simple imitations of scrolls. The superscription is sometimes doweled and glued to the cross; at other times it is set and glued into a groove cut into the top of the perpendicular beam in the manner of a crude open mortise tenon. The superscription is sometimes found with the *N* upside down, revealing the *santero's* lack of the rudiments of learning. A more striking example of simplicity is the superscription above the unusually well-carved *Christ Crucified* on the main altar of the *Santuario de Chimayó,* which has been set upside down. The frontispiece shows a Mora crucifix with the superscription repeated in the Spanish abbreviation, apparently unique.

The two beams of the cross are ordinarily made of finished wood, that is, cut to shape (sometimes with edges beveled), smoothed, covered with *yeso,* and painted. The backs of many crosses are neither *yeso*-coated nor painted, and it is not unusual to find the *Corpus yeso*-coated but unpainted on the back. Crosses with beams made of well-selected, straight branches, with bark removed and unpainted are not uncommon. The Church of San Antonio at Córdova has two crucifixes whose crosses are made in this manner. The cross is often decorated with simple patterns, as is also the loincloth. The beams are sometimes joined with a halved cross lap joint, but the more common way is with only the transverse beam cut out halfway and set over the perpendicular, leaving the surface of the transverse raised above that of the perpendicular. When the crucifix has a footrest it is sometimes set into and doweled to the Cross, and at other times it is simply doweled and glued to it.

Most New Mexican crucifixes show Our Lord with crossed feet held to the cross by one nail. The nails are often pyramidal-headed and are unusually well carved.

2. THE PREPARATION OF THE WOOD SURFACE AND THE PREPARATION AND APPLICATION OF THE YESO

After the several parts of a *bulto* were shaped and joined they were smoothed by rubbing with some abrasive, which could have been any rough stone. Pumice may have been used as a final finisher. The same operation was applied to the surface of a board destined for a flat painting. It has been said that the first coat given the wood surface was a gelatinous glue made from cow horns or animal hoofs. If this be true the coats must have been water-thin, for very few images show any evidence of such treatment. The wood itself is well prepared when one considers the poor implements used by the *santero.*

The next step was the preparation of the *yeso,* which was a combination of animal glue with *yeso,* also called *jaspe* in some parts of New Mexico. This is a native form of gypsum which was disintegrated by baking, then pulverized, dissolved in water and mixed with animal glue. The result was a sort of plaster of paris which "seems to correspond exactly to that which was used in continental European paintings for centuries."[2] After a period of drying, the *retablo* or *bulto* surface was further smoothed and shaped with tools and abrasives. These operations produced an even surface, and although very hard it was not always durable, for it flakes, peels and chips. The number of applications of the *yeso* mixture varied, dependent, it appears, upon the judgment, and perhaps the patience of the artist.

During the later years of *santo*-making, that is, from about 1870 to 1900, pulverized gypsum was mixed with *poliada,* a flour paste, and used instead of the *yeso* made with gelatinous glue. Flour-paste *yeso* was the kind used in New Mexico in earlier times to whitewash interior walls. Manifestly, this flour-paste finish is not comparable in any way to the gelatinous *yeso* finish, and is one of several features of some later *santos* which makes them decidedly inferior to the images executed during the first sixty years of the nineteenth century.

Yeso was also used to build certain features of a *bulto,* such as beards, brows, nose, lips, ears, hair, and folds in garments, beards and ears sometimes being made entirely of *yeso.* To this extent *bultos* were modeled as well as carved. *Yeso* also served to hide joints, cracks,

---

2. Gettens and Turner, *op. cit.,* p. 10.

and a multitude of errors in carving caused by poor tools or lack of skill. Cloth, either muslin, diagonal twilled cotton, and on some late figures, calico, was commonly dipped in *yeso* and wrapped around the stave framework which supported truncated bodies. This technique simplified the previous task of carving and subsequent work of shaping and smoothing, particularly where folds in garments were planned. There are, however, at least two examples of the complete carving of clothing in the wood itself on a *bulto* of *Jesús Nazareno* in the Harwood Foundation, No. 97 of that collection, and on an image of *Santa Rita*, No. 28 of the Kleijkamp and Monroe Collection, whose veil is carved out of the same wood as the head.

A fine example of the use of *yeso*-dipped cloth is seen in the garments of *Nuestra Señora de los Dolores* in a niche of the reredos on the Epistle side of the main altar at Ranchos de Taos.

Tempera colors used on a *yeso* surface penetrate well enough, so the New Mexican folk artist did not have to be concerned with the use of sizing. Boyd is of the firm opinion that the old *santeros* did not use any size, and in view of the fact that she has had occasion for many years to handle *bultos* and *retablos* day in and day out, it would seem to be rash to disagree with her.

3. THE PREPARATION AND APPLICATION OF THE TEMPERA COLORS

Mention has been made of the first scientific inquiry into the question of the pigments used by the *santeros* of New Mexico. The results of this microscopic and microchemical examination of paint specimens from thirteen *retablos*, and from the reredos and walls of the Church of San José at Laguna must serve as a starting point in any consideration of the subject. The following information on the pigments used by the folk image-makers has been secured from the Gettens and Turner study:

Blue: Indigo is not as brilliant as Prussian blue, but more resistant to alkali. It has faded only slightly from original tone. Prussian blue was found on two panels, one by Miguel Aragón, whose active period was between 1830–50. Prussian blue, an artificial pigment made by a chemical process, was imported. Indigo was imported also. Only one *retablo* from the altar screen showed the presence of blue mineral pigment, azurite (natural hydrous copper carbonate), which could be of local origin.

Black: Charcoal, carbon, lampblack.

Flesh: White lead, imported. Unpainted *yeso*.

Grey: Carbon black mixed with gypsum.

Blue grey: Carbon black mixed with gypsum.

Pinkish grey: Vermilion mixed with gypsum.

Green: Indigo observed, with other elements of possible vegetable origin. No copper greens, such as malachite or verdigris, were found. This is strange, for there are several copper ores in New Mexico.

Olive green: Isolated particles of indigo dispersed in a yellowish medium.

Pink: White lead with vermilion.

Brown: Earthy iron oxide, much like umber. Also a mixture of carbon black and vermilion. Evidence in one panel of a carbonaceous substance.

Red: Vermilion, cinnabar (red mercuric sulphide). Rare in New Mexico, but exists in commercial quantities in Arizona, California, and Mexico. An organic red, probably cochineal from Mexico. A red lead oxide pigment was found on one panel. This is artificial in origin and was probably imported. Iron oxide was identified on one panel. Red iron oxide was identified in specimens taken from the walls. When red is coarse and irregular it may be ground red mercuric sulphide.

Vermilion: Mercuric oxide. Cinnabar (red mercuric sulphide).

White: White lead, imported.

Yellow: Yellow ochre, a clay-bearing hydrous ferric oxide, identified only on one panel. Unable to determine the origin of a dull yellow found on two other panels, but may be vegetable.

Thus, Gettens and Turner were able to identify fourteen different materials from which an equal number of colors were secured.

There is little doubt that cinnabar, cochineal, indigo, Prussian blue, red lead oxide, vermilion, and white lead were importations from Mexico, the only source of imported goods for the 210 years previous to 1822, when the Santa Fe Trail was established for wagons. The remaining pigments were in all probability of local origin, and those vegetable pigments which could not be identified could also have been of local origin.

We have already seen how indigo and brazilwood were brought into New Mexico for dye purposes as early as 1665. In 1792 Father Juan Agustín de Morfí wrote that "In the mission of Zuñi . . . the Indians furnished to my companion . . . as much Prussian blue as he needed without more cost or labor than gathering it up from a mineral water which they discovered."[3] This was probably azurite, for it could not have been Prussian blue. Pedro Bautista Pino was clearer when he wrote:

> There are earths of various colors, such as blue, green, yellow, white, crimson; and in the pueblo of Zuñi there is that of azure or Prussian blue, which, according to the assurance given by the erudite and painter Don Bernardo de Miera, could be turned into a very useful commercial produce, for this earth is a perfect substitute for the paint of that color.[4]

Any of the colored earths mentioned by Pino could have been used for the making of pigments, as could also the various clays, plants and berries utilized by the Indians. While at Bent's Fort in 1846, W. H. Emory wrote:

> I had been for sometime endeavoring to obtain specimens of the materials that the Indians use to produce those brilliant hues they give to the porcupine quills with which they garnish their ornamental trappings. This morning "Old Bark" [a Cheyenne chief] brought me what I wished, the sumach berries, with which that bright red is produced, and the moss from the pine tree, that yields a yellow tint. The green dye is made from copperas [green vitriol].[5]

As there was barter between the New Mexicans, the New Mexican Indians, and the tribes to the north and east, it is possible that the sumac berry dye may have been secured this way. Where the Indians got the green vitriol is a question. Pine-tree moss was available to the *santero*.

Gettens and Turner were able to identify carbon, lampblack, and charcoal as the materials used in producing black. Other black pigments which they were unable to identify could have been the charred remains of vegetable matter, such as melon and pumpkin seeds, corn, and corncobs.

A variety of cream shades could have been made from clays.

Various shades of yellow could have been produced from the dry pollen of the flowering chamisa plant (rabbit bush), and from the pale gold and sulphur-colored clays which abound in New Mexico.

Dickey mentions the following local sources of dye pigments used in New Mexican weaving, any or all of which could have been used to make paints:[6]

Yellow from *rosillo*, the shrubby cinquefoil, related to the chamisa plant.

Tawny yellow from the tuberous roots of the *canaigra* or dock.

Tan from dock.

Yellow green from stone lichens and apple bark.

Brown from juniper bark, onion skins, and black walnut hulls.

Over six thousand species of flora have been identified and recorded in New Mexico, and over two hundred seventy-five species of min-

3. Thomas, *Antonio de Bonilla and Spanish Plans*, Vol. I, *New Spain and the Anglo American West*, Los Angeles, 1932, p. 113.

4. *Exposición sucinta*, pp. 11–12. Barreiro offers the same list in *Ojeada sobre Nuevo Méjico*, p. 22.

5. In *Report of Lieut. J. W. Abert of his Examination of New Mexico*, pp. 419–548.

6. *New Mexico Village Arts*, p. 117.

erals. Any number of these could have served to make the many colors and shades found in the decoration of *santos*. Although much of what has been said regarding the possible sources of pigments is purely speculative, it is difficult to agree with the oft-stated opinion that the *santeros* worked with a very limited palette and that they had no knowledge of mixing colors. Even the accidental mixing of two colors would have suggested the possibilities. In fact we know from the Gettens and Turner examination that carbon black and gypsum were mixed to produce grey, the same two substances to produce blue grey, vermilion with gypsum to get pinkish grey, indigo and yellow to produce olive green, white lead and vermilion for pink, carbon black and vermilion for brown.

George Wharton James, writing in 1920 after many years in New Mexico, states that the Pueblo Indians ground colored earths with yucca-fruit syrup to give it an adhesive quality.[7] Barker, and also Luhan, who have written a few lines about *santos*, transferred this technique to the *santero's* art, with other notions on the subject which Boyd very properly labels "inanities." The paints used by the *santeros* certainly have good adhesive qualities, and this could have been brought about by egg white alone, which contains casein and albumen, both used today in making glues, sizes and binders. Gettens and Turner rule out egg yolk, as suggested by Gilberto Espinosa, contending that it is too easily softened by water. It is a well-known fact, however, that either the white, the yolk, or the whole egg may be used in painting with good results. Depending upon the proportion of white to yolk, varying degrees of opacity are produced. It is this opacity, say the experts (Moreau-Vauthier, for example), which leads many students of art to mistake tempera paintings for either fresco or oil. Gettens and Turner offer the possibility of animal glue having been used as a binding material. Varnish, which was available to the *santero*, would not have been used, for the rustic image-maker would have soon discovered how quickly the combination of paint and varnish scales and peels.

The paints were applied with a brush whose bristles were made either of yucca fiber, chewed willow stick, animal hair, or several chicken feathers wrapped together with thread, leaving the tips exposed. Large areas were swabbed, with either cloth, wool, or, as the Indians did, with rabbit fur.

Pino, in the report previously cited, stated that "from the silver tree is secured a varnish which is permanent, and gives a brilliant and beautiful lustre."[8] Pino used the word *abeto*, which is the yew-leaved fir, probably the so-called Douglas fir of New Mexico. It may be that this is the varnish found on some *santos* but that the years have dulled the brilliance which Pino claimed for it. There are some *retablos* which are finished with a pine rosin varnish of poor quality which checks, cracks, peels and darkens witih age. It is easily removed, often revealing bright original colors. This may be some of Pino's "permanent" varnish.

When all of the above operations were completed, the image was finished. The last treatment might have been rubbing the image with mutton tallow applied with some non-abrasive object, such as the fingers, a piece of cloth, or wool.

Too many writers on *santos* make unqualified statements concerning the methods used in their making. It is not possible to make round assertions about many aspects of *santo*-making, for the investigator is limited to what can be observed by examination with very few additional aids. This explains the frequency of qualifications in the present study.

4. MISCELLANEOUS ASPECTS OF SANTO-MAKING

Unfortunately, the great majority of old *bultos*, perhaps seventy-five per cent, have been repainted, either to brighten the image or as an act of devotion. The removal of the new coat more often than not reveals the absence of any need for renovation. The repainters seldom adhered to the original colors.

7. *New Mexico, The Land of the Delight Makers*, p. 7.
8. Pino, *op. cit.,* p. 12.

The new paint is almost always house paint, which shows that the repainting was done, in most cases, after American occupation (1846). It has been stated that hues and brush marks indicate that the repainting was done by the same individuals. It seems more reasonable to conclude that the same colors and even brands of American house paint were available all over the Territory at the time the repainting was done. This same observation would apply to factory-made American brushes. The wide dispersion of repainted *bultos* would seem to bear this out. The existence of itinerant re-painters has been suggested. This could have been so, but considering the availability of paint, and the inept manner in which repainting was done, it would seem that this was not the case, and that the repainting of *bultos* was done by the owners themselves. *Bultos* repainted with a flat, white-oil paint may be seen today as far south as the village of Scholle, and as far north as San Luis, in southern Colorado. There are a number of instances where the repainter has changed a representation from that of one saint to another. In a case cited by Wilder, an original representation of St. Anthony of Padua was "given a beard and the tonsure and Franciscan cord painted out to produce a makeshift representation of St. Joseph."

The New Mexican wood-carver found it difficult to execute the symbols and attributes of the saints, because of their small size and the complexity, in most cases, of their design. Being small and fragile, these parts were susceptible to breakage and loss, which accounts for their absence from so many *bultos*. Small figures of the Christ Child, and objects held by the Blessed Mother, St. Joseph, and St. Anthony, are almost always missing.

Large attributes are often painted or carved in very reduced size, for to depict them in their true proportions would not only require large representations, but would detract considerably from the principal point of interest. Thus, the oxen of San Isidro are the size of jackrabbits, and the soldiers at the foot of San Acacio's cross, or the figures of Mary and John at the foot of the Cross are scarcely knee-high with relation to the main figure. As with every other feature of the *santero's* art, this is a direct descendant of European practice.

Inappropriate attributes are found on some *bultos*, the result of either an original error (which was just as common in the art of the styles), or of substitution for those lost or damaged beyond repair. Substitutions are easy to identify, for more often than not they do not match the image either in size, shape, colors, carving, or finish.

The symbols and attributes of Christ, the Virgin and the saints were made in a variety of ways and of divers materials. Crowns are carved in the ermine type with four bands curving inward and topped by a cross or knob. Pronged or crenelated types in wood are as common as the ermine type made of the same material. Tin and less frequently silver were likewise fashioned into crowns, tin coming into general use in the last half of the nineteenth century. Braided leather or twigs, and sometimes real thorns, served to make the Crown of Thorns. Wood also served to make baskets (generally held by *El Santo Niño de Atocha*), hearts, and globes, and for crosses in any type of representation. Tin and wood, and infrequently silver, were employed in the making of such symbols and attributes as swords, the scales of St. Michael, and the fish of St. Raphael. All objects of wood were generally painted.

Images of the Christ Child were often supplied with a peg to attach either permanently or temporarily to the hand or arm of His Mother or one of the saints. Sometimes larger images had holes drilled in the base for attaching to a pole, thus facilitating secure carriage in processions.

Realism has always been one of the salient characteristics of Spanish art forms everywhere, in sculpture, painting, and literature. In using bits of mica to make eyes glisten, human hair, eyelashes, and even fingernails, carved teeth and tongue, the New Mexican *santero* was only continuing a tradition which goes back to the days of Spanish eminence in polychrome sculpture. Glass eyes, which are rare in New Mexican *bultos*, seem to originate in the San Luis Valley in southern Colorado, and date from the last years of the nineteenth century. Taken from dolls, they are being placed in old *bultos* today. An unusual example is the image of Our Lady in the Museum of New Mexico, where the doll eyes add considerably to the realism of the figure. A large *bulto* of St. Anthony in the collection of Gilberto Espinosa of Albuquerque is unique in that only the arms and body are the work of a New Mexican *santero*. The head, with glass eyes, plainly belonged originally to what must have been a very attractive image of Mexican origin.[9]

Another frequent practice of the *santero* was to paint designs on the clothing of his figures. Sometimes this was any symmetrical arrangement of variously shaped designs, at others it is a plain effort to imitate the *estofado*, or painted relievos on gilt ground, of baroque statuary throughout the Christian world. There are instances also of the application of embroidery to the cotton loincloth of Christ, as on the *Man of Sorrows*, from Abiquiú, in the Taylor Museum.

Still another practice was to place images under canopies or in cases formed by a canopy with sides. This furniture is called a *nicho* (niche) in New Mexico. In view of the fact that they were used to house a *bulto* on a wall, the name is very appropriately chosen, for they are nothing other than portable niches. *Nichos* are made of either wood or tin, tin coming into general use, as in the making of symbols and attributes, after American occupation. Oil cans brought in by American troops were used in the fashioning of all sorts of objects, including religious ornaments and furniture. The *bulto* of *The Crowning with Thorns* in the Taylor Museum is set in a niche made from a can with a Continental Oil Company mark.[10]

Wooden *nichos* are of all shapes and var-iously designed, some made up of only a canopy upheld by two or more posts or a back. They are sometimes decorated with carving, and are always painted. Decorating with straw mosaic was also used, although infrequently. Sometimes little angels or a dove, either painted or in the round, added further decoration. Tin *nichos* lined with wallpaper, or made up of tin frames with glass to form the sides, are also quite common.

A number of *retablos* are found where the artist has followed the practice of the painter of chests by placing a brand mark on horses. Sometimes this mark is only the initial or initials of the painter, as in the case of the *Flight into Egypt* panel by José Rafael Aragón of the Kleijkamp and Monroe Collection, which has only an *A*. Again, this mark may be just a fancy curlicue, as on the horse of *Santiago* by the Chili Painter in the Museum of New Mexico, a skin painting.

In the course of the development of Christian art, certain colors or color combinations became symbolic, and to some extent standardized in association with certain saints. New Mexican *santeros* were not too consistent in using the colors found on their models, deviating, it seems, when their palette was limited. It should be mentioned that the blue habits always shown on representations of Franciscan saints in New Mexican folk art show the true color of the friar's habit in New Mexico.[11]

---

9. Repro. in Espinosa, "New Mexican Santos," Part I, *New Mexico*, XXXI (March, 1935), 10.

10. Repro. in RFA, Pl. 29, and erroneously identified as Job.

11. This is not because of the blue habits of the Franciscans of the Province of Zacatecas, Mexico, as has been stated. The New Mexican friars belonged to the Province of the Holy Gospel in Mexico City. It is not known exactly why the New Mexican friars wore blue. The color and shape of the Franciscan habit were not prescribed by St. Francis in his Rule. To attain uniformity, dark brown or chestnut was prescribed by Pope Leo XIII in 1898.

6. Retablo Painters

ABOUT THE MIDDLE of the eighteenth century amateur carvers and painters undertook the execution of sacred images. Using European and Mexican images as models, they worked strictly as imitators and copyists. This group, apparently very small in numbers, is the one that immediately preceded the craftsmen from the villages and hamlets, who began their efforts about the third quarter of the eighteenth century. Around 1785, with a leeway of five years one way or the other, direct copying and imitation began to decline. As Dickey says, "A spirit of original design entered New Mexican art, and by 1800 the tradition was fixed in regional techniques and characteristic motifs." From this date until about 1855, New Mexico had her golden age of religious folk art. After 1855 until around 1880 there is, excepting for four painters, a general decline, the rural artists making a gallant but progressively more futile effort down to the very end of the century. Throughout their history, however, *santos* are characterized by conventional representations with respect to the use of historical and traditional symbols and attributes. Sophisticated models also continued to be observed by the folk image-makers as shown in the conventional poses of figures in both *retablos* and *bultos*.

The carving and painting of images was not restricted to any one section of northern New Mexico, but workers were particularly active in Río Arriba and Taos counties. Much fine work was done much farther south in the Lower Rio Grande Valley, in and around Tomé, Valencia, and Adelino. The finest examples come from the homes and chapels in and around Arroyo Hondo, Taos, Córdova, Abiquiú, Santa Cruz, Chamisal, Chimayó, Trampas, El Rito, Canjilón, La Madera, and other tiny hamlets, from across the Sangre de Cristo Range in Mora, and across the New Mexican border in the south-central part of Colorado, many of the Colorado images being of New Mexican origin.

A basis for the opinion that the *santero* was sometimes an itinerant craftsman is found in the wide distribution of images of the same type, and by the same artists. Some of the finest works of two of the most prolific panel painters (José Rafael Aragón and the Chili Painter, *infra*) are found today in altar-screens installed in village chapels along a thirty-mile stretch of the Chimayó Valley, namely, at Santa Cruz, Chimayó, Córdova, Trampas, and Ranchos de Taos. Also, we have the word of Avelino Velázquez, a younger son of Juan Ramón Velázquez (*infra*), that his father had enough commissions to make it worth his while to take along his family and live from three to six months in a place while he executed the *bultos* agreed upon. However, Don Avelino's statement cannot be taken at its face value, for only a handful of *bultos* have so far been identified as the work of his father.

Several *santeros* were unquestionably full-time professionals, working either on orders or to replenish their stock during the months of difficult travel, and taking to the byways in comfortable season to seek buyers or to make deliveries. They could have worked both at home and at the place where a commission was to be fulfilled.

Only two panel painters signed some of their work, which makes the task of identifying the remainder of their work a facile one. As for the rest, the study of styles is the principal means of establishing authorship. The most competent in the work of identification is E. Boyd, Curator of Spanish Colonial Art, Museum of New Mexico. Of the twelve panel painters to whom specific *retablos* can be assigned, ten have been isolated by her. These twelve painters, with the probable dates of their activity, will be considered individually.

1. THE LAGUNA PAINTER, 1775–1800

Some fifty miles west of Albuquerque is the Indian pueblo of San José de Laguna, established as a mission in 1699. The church, constructed in 1706, displays in its reredos the masterpiece of all *santero* art (Pl. 11). The artist who executed this altar-screen is not known by name, and is referred to as the Laguna Painter.

It is certain that the four panels of the Laguna reredos were not painted anywhere near the time when the church was erected, for this was about sixty years too early for the advent of folk painting. The Laguna altar-screen was not there in 1776 when Domínguez made his inventory, so it would appear sound to set upon the years 1776–1800 as those when the Laguna Painter worked, and fix the date sometime between 1790 and 1800 when the reredos at Laguna was painted and installed. We may also be sure that the four panels were copies from sophisticated models, for the renditions of the Trinity, St. John Nepomucene, St. Joseph and St. Barbara reflect every detail of traditional European representations, down to the scapulary medal worn by St. John as a member of the Order of Canons Regular of St. Augustine.

Three questions persist concerning the Laguna reredos: How can we explain the earliness of this example of superior folk painting? How did it happen that the most outstanding of folk panels were set up, and apparently executed, so far from the area of *santero* concentration? Why has it not been possible to isolate at least one other *retablo* by the Laguna Painter?

There is an answer to the first question: The Laguna reredos constitutes a perfect link between the folk artists who slavishly, laboriously, and with only a modicum of success, copied and imitated the art of the schools, and the absolutely untutored craftsmen who make up the main body of New Mexican *santeros*. The Laguna Painter was nothing other than a superb copyist of sophisticated originals. A stylistic detail of the work of the Laguna Painter that indicates his position as an amateur is found in the "dislocated" or elongated thumbs and the generally simplified hands of his figures, so remindful of those drawn by the folk artists of a later day, especially those of the Chili Painter.

The last two questions may be considered simultaneously: The Laguna panels are not the first, nor perhaps the last, fruit of their author's brush, for they betray a hand of some experience. It is not logical to think that this altar-screen is the only piece he ever executed. Thus, it may well be that he was not a New Mexican at all, but either a "floater" from Zacatecas, Durango, or Chihuahua, or a Franciscan who remained at Laguna just long enough to execute a direly needed ornament. We may have in the Laguna Painter another, but competent, Fr. García, the Franciscan who tried with little success, sometime between March 19, 1773, and November 28, 1775, to furnish the image-starved church at Laguna with the two *bultos* so severely criticized by Domínguez in 1776.[1] These possibilities would also account for the high quality of the reredos and that it is so far away from the Upper Rio Grande Valley, where the majority of *santeros* were developed. He scarcely could have been from the Tomé district, for no *retablos* in this area in any way resemble the work of the Laguna Painter.

The same materials used by later *santeros* were employed to make the Laguna panels, which show a confident brush of extensive practice. The dominant colors are red, various shades of grey, blue, and black, with certain areas appearing as a pinkish grey. The Laguna reredos is further notable for the achievement of a third dimension, far beyond that of most *santero* paintings.[2]

2. THE CALLIGRAPHIC PAINTER, 1800–30

Dr. W. S. Stallings, Jr. suggested the name which Boyd has used to identify this panel painter, who worked during the classic period of *santería*. The type panel employed by her to isolate this artist is a representation of St. Anthony in the Cady Wells Collection. The Calligraphic Painter did not submit entirely to prototypes, as shown by the marked originality so often displayed in his compositions. His style embraces very particular and easily recognizable characteristics, most prominent among these being "the nervous line," the stylized hands, the long, slender noses, and often almond-shaped eyes of his figures. He sometimes drew the nimbi of the Christ Child and a saint together, joining them to form a figure 8, as on Harwood 42 representing St. Joseph, and sometimes with a sort of buttonhole stitching around the inside of the circle or circles, as on No. 48 of the same collection depicting Christ Crucified (Pl. 12). The figures of his personages are finely drawn, with loosely folded hands and delicately outlined fingers. The long nose drawn in a continuous line with one or both eyebrows, and tiny mouth are details generally found on his panels in addition to those already mentioned. On images of the Virgin the balls of the hands are frequently quite enlarged. His *retablos* may be further described as exhibiting original and imaginative ornamentation in the form of incised borders, stylized trees and shrubs, and tiled floors.

A representation of St. Teresa, inscribed *Santísima Teresa*, of the Boyd Collection, is unique in *santero* art in that the figure is done in the traditional tempera colors but on a sheet of rag paper which is tipped onto the upper three-quarters of a *yeso*-coated pine panel.[3] The representation of *St. Raphael and the Boy Tobias*, Carroll SR-308, shows the fond-

ness of the Calligraphic Painter for complex ornamentation, sometimes bordering on confusion. His representations of the Crucifixion are always interesting by reason of the flowing lines of the *Corpus*, the invariably downcast eyes, somewhat in the manner of the Oriental Painter (*infra*), and the elaborate pouf drawn as part of the loincloth. It is apparent that he used woodcuts and engravings as models, especially of the type put out during the heyday of romanticism.[4]

Other representative *retablos* by the Calligraphic Painter are: Carroll, *Our Lady of the Cape*,[5] and SR-309 of the same collection representing *St. Raymond Nonnatus*. Fiske Day, *Christ Crucified*.[6] Spanish Colonial Arts Society No. 4, *Christ Crucified*. Wells R-15, *Veronica's Veil* (Pl. 13), R. 68, *Our Lady of Sorrows*, R-70, *St. Clare of Assisi*, and R-136, *Sts. Martinian and Processus*. Barton 9, *Our Lady of Mt. Carmel*, 10, *Our Lady of Guadalupe*, 11, *Veronica's Veil*, 12, *Our Lady of San Juan de los Lagos*, and 13, *St. Raymond Nonnatus*.[7] Harwood 18, *St. Anthony of Padua*, 42, *St. Joseph*, 48, *Christ Crucified*, 29, *Our Lady of Protection*, inscribed SRA NUESTRA *de lo* PATROCINIO,[8] and 80, *Our Lady of Sorrows*. Taylor Museum, *Christ Crucified*,[9] and Hispanic Society of America Panels, *Christ Crucified* (Pl. 30).

3. THE CHILI PAINTER, 1815–40

During the height of the golden age of *santo*-making there worked in the villages of southwestern Rio Arriba County and southern Taos County, traditionally Chamita and Abi-

1. *See* Domínguez, *The Missions of New Mexico, 1776,* pp. 184, 333.
2. Repro. in color in *Life* (January 16, 1956), 48–49.
3. Repro. on cover of EP, 58, 6 (June, 1951); *see* same issue for Boyd, "An Early New Mexican Watercolor," 163–64.
4. *See* Boyd, "The Source of Certain Elements in Santero Paintings of the Crucifixion," EP, 58, 8 (August, 1951), 235–36.
5. Repro. in EP, 57, 3 (March, 1950), 84.
6. Repro. on cover of EP, 58, 8 (August, 1951).
7. All Barton panels repro. in ABC.
8. The *Our Lady of Protection* panel is one of the twelve "missing" Harwood *retablos*.
9. Repro. in RFA, Pl. 64.

quiú, a *santero* whose personality is surrounded by the vaguest sort of lore. The fact that his panels are all hand-adzed allows the placing of a limit on his period of activity, for after American occupation (1846) milled commercial boards become common.

The old folk of southern Taos and Rio Arriba counties recall, according to Boyd, that this *santero's* name was something like "Molleño," or "Monillo." Neither of these names is known in New Mexico today, and they do not appear in any of the records examined. One Juan José Moreño appears in a Santa Fe record of 1764. Dr. W. W. Stallings, Jr. claims evidence that the Chili Painter's name was Ignacio Durán.

Boyd has named this *santero* "the Chili Painter," seeing in certain scalloped motifs forms resembling chili pods, with which the artist was wont to fill the bottom and sometimes other spaces in his later style panels. The early style of the Chili Painter is conventional and realistic, well exemplified by the eight panels of the Evans Collection in the Denver Art Museum, A-136 of that collection. The influence of sophisticated models is plainly visible in this as in his other early panels. Elongated figures and the use of white dots are also common to his early *retablos*. The Chili Painter's outlines are black and backgrounds white, with shades of red, light blue, light green, and yellows making up the remainder of his palette. His pigments sometimes show the presence of *tierra amarilla,* a micaceous yellow earth common to various sections of Rio Arriba County, notably around the town named after this substance. Also representative of his early period is the reredos in the east transept of the Church of San Francisco at Ranchos de Taos, the Boyd panel of *Our Lady of Sorrows,* Wells R-68 of the same subject, and Barton 17 of *St. Anthony of Padua.*[10]

The three-quarters' view of the head is the most noticeable feature of the Chili Painter's late style, further characterized by greater ease of execution and evenness of composition. The three-quarters' face is done with a single line, nearly always diagonal, as on his *St. Anthony* of the Hispanic Society of America

Panels (Pl. 30), but sometimes perpendicular, as on his *St. Joseph* of the same set. Again, it may be a sweeping curve, as on Wells R-96 of *St. Gertrude* and Carroll 415 of *Our Lady of Sorrows.* Two or three sweeps of the brush, resulting in a heavy flourish, satisfied the Chili Painter's conception of a full beard. Although he was capable of drawing graceful hands, as shown by a number of his early paintings, his later panels regularly show these members as little more than awkward scrawls, with gigantic, "dislocated" thumbs (Pl. 15). His hands may have from three to six fingers, and on the representation of *Our Lady of Guadalupe,* Harwood No. 96, the right hand has four fingers and the left hand three. The Chili Painter drew feet either in simple outline or as solid black blotches. More often than not they appear stubby, clublike, and twisted. It seems that his only point of anatomical interest in his later years was the face. Some of his panels have solid red corners, and these are thought by Boyd to belong to his last years of activity.

Generally speaking, the Chili Painter's drawing is absolutely flat, but this does not always apply to the clothing of his figures, which often shows an effort to achieve a third dimension, inspired, in his early panels, by academic models. He surrounded his figures very often with decorative motifs of one sort or another, such as simple drapes, variously designed ovals, corners filled with scallops, and light or heavy outlines of lifeless flowers. He very frequently drew a solid, chestlike piece at one side or at both sides of a central figure. This piece is sometimes topped by a disc and is of almost columnar proportions. Within the outline of this piece the above-mentioned scallops usually appear.

Quite inconsistent in the care with which he painted, much of the Chili Painter's late work is crude, elementary, and naïve: Harwood 81, *Our Lady of San Juan de los Lagos;* Carroll R-116, *Christ Crucified;* Fiske Day R-23, *Christ Carrying His Cross* (Pl. 15); Fiske Day R-3, *St. Michael;* Wells R-30, *San*

---

10. Repro. in ABC.

Acacio; Kleijkamp and Monroe 78, *St. Dominic*; and Harwood 10, *St. Jerome*.

The reredos in the church at Talpa is by the Chili Painter. In almost pristine condition, it is in what Boyd calls the free style of his middle period. It is inscribed:

Se yso y se pinto en este año de 1828 a debosyon de Bernardo Luxan este oratorio de Misa de San Juan.

This chapel of St. John was made and painted in this year of 1828 at the pious behest of Bernardo Luxán.

In the right-hand panel of the middle tier of a reredos in the church at Ranchos de Taos the Chili Painter presents a bearded male figure in short, capelike garment hanging loosely over his shoulders. The legs are shown in what appears like white, tight-fitting trousers, with a double row of buttons running along the shins from ankles to knees. He holds three nail-like objects in his right hand and a palm and Cross in his left hand. Here is another case where the Chili Painter is aberrant enough to posit an interesting problem of identification. The task here is to establish the identity of the three objects in the saint's right hand, which are taken to be nails or spikes. Their flat heads rule out arrows, objects with which the New Mexican was thoroughly and often painfully familiar, and which he could easily have represented.[11]

Also by the Chili Painter are the principal reredos and the reredos on the east wall farthest from the altar in the Santuario at Chimayó. The first contains five symbolic paintings; the second, four panels representing saints and one of the so-called *Árbol de la Cruz*, known in English as the Cross and Winding Sheet.

The Chili Painter depicted almost every saint enjoying popularity in New Mexico, and some not too common in New Mexican folk art, such as St. Roch, St. Giles, and the Prophet Elias. His symbolic paintings, as shown on the main reredos at Chimayó,[12] are always well done. His *Sacred Heart*, Carroll SR-417, is most attractive. He is also the author of two of the four known *santero*

paintings on animal skins, *St. Francis of Assisi*, in the Brooklyn Museum, and *St. James the Greater*, in the Museum of New Mexico. One of the most prolific of all *santeros*, his panels may be found in almost any collection.

4. EL NIÑO PERDIDO PAINTER, 1820–40

Nothing whatever is known concerning the identity of this panel painter, the above name being the one given him by Boyd after the panel depicting The Lost Christ Child, B87–269 in the Museum of New Mexico, which was used by her as a type example of his style. As in the case of most *santeros*, there is every evidence that he worked from conventional representations of the saints. His hand-adzed boards and other features permit one to settle upon the years 1820–40 as the approximate time of his activity.[13]

The style of this painter has a number of characteristics which render identification of his work a facile task. Principal ones are the curly, pointed lobes, the close-set eyes, and the down-slanted eyebrows of most of his figures. He did not crowd his panels, leaving clean, open spaces to accent the figure, even when there are more than one on the *retablo*. Panels by El Niño Perdido Painter are quite rare. Besides the Lost Christ Child panel, mention can be made of Barton 21 representing the *Christ Child of Atocha*,[14] Harwood 31 of *St. Gertrude*,[15] another Atocha in the Museum of New Mexico, and *Our Lady of Mount Carmel* (Pl. 16). The three heads in profile which appear on the Carmel panel are not common in *santero* art, although such drawings are found on the bases of *bultos* in the Church of San Antonio at Córdova, and on a few panels by other *santeros*, notably José Aragón.

11. The following possibilities are suggested: St. Bernard of Alcira, St. Quintin, St. Felician, St. Primus, and even St. Longinus, as Three Nails are a Passion symbol.
12. Repro. in MMNM, 115.
13. *See* Boyd, "El Niño Perdido Painter," EP, 57, 1 (Jan., 1950), 11–12.
14. Repro. as No. 21 in AIB.
15. This is another of the "missing" Harwood panels.

5. JOSÉ ARAGÓN OF CHAMISAL, 1820–40

The village of Chamisal is in the southernmost part of Taos County, in the heart of the Sangre de Cristo Range. It is a rather somber little place compared to the more cheerful hamlets of rural New Mexico. The dilapidated *camposantos*, cemeteries, in this section alone suffice to remind one of "The short and simple annals of the poor." Seldom mentioned in literature, and less frequently visited, even by New Mexicans, this *placita* gave to New Mexico one of the two folk painters known to us by name without benefit of conjecture, legend, or local tradition. His name, as shown by his signature on five panels, was José Aragón, and the place of his residence is stated in two inscriptions, one dated 1827 and the other 1831. José Aragón worked from conventional representations, either Mexican or European, as did most *santeros*.

With the certainty that by the time these words go to press other *retablos* signed or otherwise inscribed by José Aragón will be discovered, here is a list of his ten panels thus identified:

1. Inscription: *El Patriarca San Jose. Jose Argon. Año de 1823.* Dimensions 7½" × 12". The Taylor Museum.
2. Inscription: *S. Geronimo Se pinto el dia Junio el Año 1827 en la   Señora de Guadalupe.* Dimensions: 8¾" × 14½". Meem Collection.
3. Inscription: *Se pinto el Año de 1830 el dia 21 de Julio.* Dimensions: 9½" × 16". Meem Collection.
4. Inscription: *Santa Barbara. Se pinto en el Chamisal A 21 de Julio de 1830 Año Jose Aragon.* Dimensions 9½" × 16". Meem Collection.[16]
5. Inscription: *SANTA ROSALIA se pinto a 22 de julio deste Año de 1830 en el Chamisal Jose Aragon.* Dimensions: 6¼" × 9½". Barton Collection.[17]
6. Only legible part of inscription: *de 1831.* Dimensions: 6⁵⁄₁₆" × 9⅛". Wells Collection. St. Jerome.
7. Inscription: *Nᵃ Sᵃ de San Juan de los Lagos.* Dimensions: 6¼" × 8¹⁵⁄₁₆". Wells Collection. Pl. 17.
8. Inscription: *N. S. Del Refugio Se Pinto Aragon.* Dimensions: 6¾" × 11¼". Boyd Collection.
9. Inscription: *Santa Dul. V.B.I.N.A.*[18] Dimensions: 5" × 7¾". Historical Society of New Mexico Collection.
10. Inscription:

    ORACION AL AN gel de nuestra guarda. Dios que con Divina providencia provisteso por luz del camino de los Angeles: dadme gracia con que asi del de me guarda; que pudiera ser en todo tienpo de mi vida con el por Jesus Cristo nuestro Señor Amen, se pinto Al   de Marzo de 1835 en la escribanía de José Aragon.[19]

    Dimensions 22" × 11¼", not counting shell at top. Wells Collection.

The dominant tone of most of the above panels is brown. Don José was given to filling spaces with cross-hatched patterns, sometimes incised, as on the 1827 San Jerónimo panel. This cross-hatching points to Mexican models, for it is well known that the painters of votive and other pictures on metal in Mexico during the eighteenth century imitated the cross-hatching which was such a prominent feature of seventeenth century European and Spanish-American woodcuts. Although brown is

---

16. Repro. in SSM, Figure 5.

17. Repro. in ABC, No. 1.

18. This is the folk artist's and the New Mexican rural spelling of *Santa* Liduvina, really *La Beata* Liduvina, Blessed Lydwina of Schiedam. *See* Boyd, "The Herder's Kit," EP, 59, 4 (April, 1952), 103. *Also,* Espinosa, "A Little Dutch Girl Far from Home," EP, 61, 3 (March, 1954), 70–73.

19. Due to defacement, and deterioration in spots, this inscription is not completely legible. However, it is a relatively easy task to supply the missing words and phrases, for this is but a New Mexican paraphrasing of the prayer for the Feast of the Guardian Angels, October 2. This would be close to the complete New Mexican original: *Dios, que con divina providencia proveíste para luz del camino de la vida la protección de los ángeles; dadme gracia con que así me valga de la protección del de mi Guarda; que pudiera estar con él en todo tiempo de mi vida. Por Jesucristo Nuestro Señor. Amén.* In English translation: "God, who with divine providence provided as a light along the way of life the protection of the angels; give me the grace with which I might avail myself of the protection of my Guardian Angel; and that I might remain close to him every moment of my life; through Jesus Christ Our Lord. Amen." The folk artist used the word *escribanía* (office, study) to mean "workshop."

the dominant tone of José Aragón's panels, his color schemes include red, dull red, blue, black, and, less extensively, yellow and light green. His panels are further recognizable by his indication of tiled paving in the foreground, always without perspective, by delicate outlines which betray the caution with which he painted, by his lettering of the names of saints, and by the single arc and dot with which he satisfied his idea of the human eye. Tiled paving, however, is not exclusive to José Aragón's panels, for it is also found on those of the Calligraphic Painter. Don José's *Santa Barbara* is representative of his manner of drawing architectual structures and also typifies his frequent tendency to crowd his figures with all sorts of ornamentation. His *Nuestra Señora del Refugio* of the Boyd Collection shows this tendency in the form of an arch of large, unrealistic flowers around the figures of the Virgin and Child. The faces of his personages are rather attractive, and his rendition of raiment is quite pleasing.

Harwood Nos. 3, 23, 55, and 95, representing *St. Ignatius Loyola*, *Our Lady of Refuge*, *St. John Nepomucene*, and *Our Lady of the Rosary*, respectively, are by José Aragón. No. 55 is predominantly brown, with less extensive use of Don José's other colors, and with three cross-hatched patterns at the top. No. 95 is done in brown, red, and light green, with the same patterns at the top. No. 23 is exceptionally well composed, the borders and cherubs in profile being very characteristic. Kleijkamp and Monroe 77 represents Our Lady of the Annunciation,[20] and Barton 2 depicts *St. Barbara*,[21] much like the signed St. Barbara, even to the construction of the tower.

A delicate and charming conception of Our Lady of San Juan de los Lagos, Wells R-67, shows the quality and character of José Aragón's brush as well as any of his panels. R-10 of the same collection is indicative of his more simple manner. The reredos on the west wall of the Santuario at Chimayó, made up of fifteen panels, are by him. His work is typical *santero* art, as far away from slavish imitation as any of these artists ever arrived.

6. JOSÉ RAFAEL ARAGÓN OF CÓRDOVA, 1830–50

There is a New Mexican *retablo* representing St. Cajetan[22] (Pl. 19) which bears the following inscription:

S CAHETANO   ARAGon
            JoSe RAFel

This signed panel is in excellent condition and thus permits one to observe in the greatest detail the technical characteristics and artistic mannerisms of the painter. Even a superficial examination of Harwood 22, depicting Our Lady of Solitude, shows that the author is also José Rafael Aragón. Beyond facial details, the same colors and the identical symbols and attributes are the outstanding marks of similarity.

Some years ago the late Frank Applegate of Santa Fe announced the name of a *santero* which was given to him by old residents of Córdova, a village just north of the southwestern border of Rio Arriba County. The villagers identified this folk artist as Miguel Aragón, and attributed certain panels to him. A study of a number of other panels made it an easy task to ascribe them to the same artist. However, a comparison of all the panels attributed to Miguel with the *St. Cajetan* and the *Our Lady of Solitude* panels discloses that they were all done by the same painter. In the light of the fact that the Cajetan panel is signed, it follows that the artist for all of these *retablos* was José Rafael Aragón, and not Miguel Aragón.

José Rafael is one of the great New Mexican folk panel painters. There is no record or tradition to indicate that he was related to either José Aragón or Miguel Aragón (*infra*), but the three could easily have been of the same clan, for Córdova and Chamisal, the

---

20. Repro. in APR, p. 26.

21. Repro. in ABC, Fig. 1.

22. This panel is from the Spinden Collection, and is reproduced as Slide No. SA65 of Dr. Block Color Reproductions, The Museum of Modern Art Library, New York. A very unsatisfactory article on these slides is in Vol. VIII, No. 2, of *College Art Journal*.

former the traditional residence of José Rafael and Miguel, and the latter village the known home of José, are only some twelve miles apart.[23]

José Rafael drew faces, particularly eyes, with a marked expression of sadness. The upper eyelid, along with the forehead, is almost always white, with the lower eyelid painted a greyish tone. A superior example of this is his inscribed panel of St. Michael the Archangel,[24] No. A.5.52–89 of the Museum of New Mexico. The headdress of the saint is here most unusual, being little more than a decoration and indicating some very idealized model. The cheeks of his saints are generally tinted pink. His backgrounds are usually white, but some have red and others brown backgrounds speckled with *tierra amarilla*. His outlines are black, filled in with reds, clear yellows, pale blues, greyish browns, light browns, dark browns, and various shades of green. Spaces not occupied by figures are decorated in a variety of ways, often with dots of various colors, as on Wells R-15 representing St. Jerome, whose fineness of line was made possible by a smoothly prepared surface. Frequently spaces are filled with drapery and sometimes with red flowers, as on Harwood 37 of *Our Lady of Solitude*. As with other *santeros*, objects are introduced into open spaces which are sometimes difficult to identify, particularly when the life or special virtues of the saint are not of any help. An example of this is the gratelike object to the right of St. Joseph on Harwood 82. The thought might occur to one that some of these unrecognizable objects were merely attempts to decorate, but on more than one occasion they have been found appropriate. The old *santeros* knew what they were about.

The three upper panels of the reredos in the chapel of the Third Order of St. Francis in the Church of the Holy Cross at Santa Cruz, depicting St. Raphael, St. Michael, and The Holy Trinity, are fine examples of the work of José Rafael, as are also the reredos from the Durán Chapel (Pl. 21), those from the Church of Our Lady of Mt. Carmel, Llano Quemado, now in the Museum of New Mexico, those of the principal altar in the Church of San Antonio at Córdova, the reredos at Llano Quemado, and the six panels forming the reredos on the east wall closest to the altar in the *Santuario* at Chimayó.

The *Flight into Egypt*, Kleijkamp and Monroe 72,[25] is José Rafael's masterpiece. The confused mass of figures on the bottom of this panel is somewhat rivaled in its disorder by another *retablo* of this artist, which before the Second World War was in Germany, but the whereabouts of which at the present time is unknown. It contains eleven different figures, symbols, and attributes, unrelated and haphazardly disposed. On the positive side, the *Flight into Egypt* panel is sensitively executed, and is plainly an original conception based upon familiarity with the story. St. Joseph leads the horselike donkey, an angel hovers behind the beast, and the Virgin Mother rides sidesaddle with her left hand on her breast nursing the Child. All figures have the typical, sad expression of José Rafael's personages. A number of symbols and one attribute have been employed, occupying areas of the panel above the figures: The Lamb, Three Loaves, The Chalice, The Dove, The Stag of St. Eustace with a Cross between its antlers, and the Sacred Heart. José Rafael loved to tell stories through symbols and attributes, which may have given him a reputation for erudition among his simple and pious people. Following the practice of the painters of wooden chests, the artist has placed his brand, *A*, on the rump of the donkey.

Besides Nos. 22, 37, 62 and 82, the Harwood Foundation has ten panels by José Rafael: 9, *St. Rosalia;* 24, *The Holy Child of Atocha;* 36, *The Child Jesus;* 40, *Our Lady of Solitude;* 61, *St. James the Greater;* 64, *The Holy Family;* 69, *St. Michael;* 70, *St. Barbara;* 77, *Our Lady of San Juan de los*

23. One Felix de Aragón was in Santa Fe in 1694. "Perhaps the Rio Arriba Aragons are descended from him." Chávez, *Origins of New Mexico Families,* Santa Fe, [1954], 123.

24. The original was an engraving with the saint's motto backwards, which the folk artist copied ⊃ΟΝΙ2Ν LΟΕΝ2, for *Quis ut Deus,* "Who is like unto God," the meaning of Michael.

25. Repro. in APR, p. 25.

Lagos; and 78, *The Crowning with Thorns.*

The Barton Collection contains the following panels by this artist: No. 3, *St. Ferdinand* (the lettering of which is remarkably like that on the Spinden *St. Cajetan* of Pl. 19); 4, a *Starred Madonna* which appears to be some local advocation of Our Lady of Solitude; 5, *Our Lady of Sorrows;* 6, *The Holy Child of Atocha.*[26] The Fiske Day Collection has three exceptionally fine panels: R-27, *St. Francis of Assisi;* R-30, *St. Raymond Nonnatus;* and R-26, *St. Hyacinth* (Aug. 17). Also in the Museum of New Mexico are Nos. A.5.52-64, *St. Michael;* and Wells R-128, *God the Father.*

The Mabel Dodge Luhan article of 1925 reproduces two beautiful panels by José Rafael, one depicting *The Holy Family,* and the other *Christ at the Pillar.*

7. MIGUEL ARAGÓN OF CÓRDOVA, 1835-55

The panel painter heretofore known as Miguel Aragón was in reality José Rafael Aragón of the same village. Also working in Córdova or vicinity, and between the approximate dates 1835-55, was a panel painter who took the works of José Rafael as models. Up to the present writing he had been known as "the Follower of Miguel Aragón." Considering that Miguel has been shown to have been José Rafael, it is believed that the so-called "Follower" was Miguel himself.

The character of Miguel's panels show that he was not an apprentice, but merely an imitator of José Rafael, and that they did not work in the same shop or home. The lifeless cast of Miguel's colors as opposed to the lively pigments of José Rafael is enough evidence to insist upon this view. Miguel sometimes used milled boards, indicating that he was a younger man than José Rafael and that he probably took up the craft of image-making later.

Where José Rafael fully outlines the upper and lower eyelids, Miguel seldom drew the lower lid at all, and drew the upper lid with one line with little if any shading. These details are found on Barton Nos. 7 and 8, the

first being a representation of St. Acacius and the second of St. Raphael.[27] The small, stylized trees with which Miguel often decorated the lower corners of his panels (not unusual with other painters) are present on Harwood 45 depicting St. Joseph. This collection has at least three other panels by Miguel: 68, *The Font of Life;* 8, *Our Lady of Sorrows* (Pl. 22); and 90, *St. Gertrude the Great.* Two other well-known panels by him are Spanish Colonial Arts Society L.3.51-8, *St. Peter;* and Wells R-42, *The Holy Child of Atocha.* To these we may add the unusual representation of Melchisedech, Michael and Moses illustrated in Pl. 20.

8. A FOURTH ARAGÓN, 1835-60

The panel depicting St. Ignatius Loyola reproduced in Pl. 23 has been used by Boyd as a type example of the work of a painter whose three known panels are all representations of the founder of the Society of Jesus. The saint depicted is identified mainly through a comparison of the panel with the two inscribed panels by the Dot-Dash Painter, one reproduced in Pl. 25. A close study of the works of the three Aragóns advocates the idea that the Fourth Aragón was a constant observer of their work and that he took his inspiration from them. The similarities existing between the characteristics of these four men is indicative of a definite relationship and reciprocal influence, and this is the principal reason why Boyd suggests the probability that the painter now being considered was in reality a Fourth Aragón. If this is true, then our panel painter was from the same area as the others, that is, from around Santa Cruz, Córdova and Chamisal, and that he worked a few years later. The circumstance that he was so partial, as far as is known, to representing St. Ignatius rather supports this notion relating to his active years, for the Jesuit saint was not popular in New Mexico until sometime after the Franciscans started to leave in 1821. In fact, as the century wore on, St. Ignatius became more

26. All repro. in ABC.

27. Repro. in ABC, where they are identified as the work of the Follower of Miguel Aragón.

popular, and toward the last of the nineteenth century some of the most elementary and naïve *retablos* are representations of him.

The panel reproduced in Pl. 23, has an enamel-like quality that is noticeable even in the photograph. The prominence of the hairline, the widow's peak, the clear rendition of eye details, the divided beard, the cupid's bow mouth, and, especially, the enlarged index finger, are features which conspire to identify the principal trademarks of the Fourth Aragón.

The Taylor Museum possesses a St. Ignatius panel by the Fourth Aragón. Another is Harwood 3, notable for its attractive, circular shape with three shells at the top and at the bottom. Still another is reproduced in the Luhan article previously cited. The fifth representation of St. Ignatius by our *santero* would be the most delightfully amusing in all New Mexican folk art were it not for evidence that the ludicrous inscription is not a part of the original painting. St. Ignatius is here disposed as in all New Mexican depictions of him, except that in the oval which surrounds the figure the following inscription appears: BIER HER BIER HER ODER ICH FALL'UM, which translated is "Bring me beer, bring me beer, before I fall down." The association of the first lines of an old and well-known German drinking song with an image of St. Ignatius Loyola was at first glance more than mystifying. There are, however, a number of reasons which indicate that the legend is a later addition, and not by the hand of the folk artist:

1. The lettering is of a style entirely different from that of any other panel by the Fourth Aragón.

2. The lettering is squeezed into the outlines of the oval, indicating that the space was not intended for an inscription.

3. New Mexican panel painters slavishly copied inscriptions, always in either Spanish or Latin, even perpetuating an original error in some cases. The German inscription on the panel under consideration is too incongruous to accept as having been on any image of the founder of the Society of Jesus.

4. New Mexican *santeros* were surprisingly consistent in the employment of basic iconographic elements in traditional manners. Of the nine representations of St. Ignatius in New Mexican folk art so far studied by the author, all are similarly disposed, and this is the only one with a German inscription.

5. The last reason for considering the inscription the later addition of a flippant mind is a scientific one, and is the finding of E. Boyd. Quoting from notes made in the early spring of 1952, she writes:

> The panel had in the past been badly flaked and was patched with modern patching plaster which has again begun to flake away. Halo and background were coated with a strong wash of transparent Prussian blue water color which washed off in acetone, exposing the original white halo and the original softer indigo background. The lettering in the border also proved to be soluble in acetone. This might indicate either that it was a retouching of old defaced letters, or simply a later addition. *Santero* tempera never dissolves under the usual cleaning solvents, except in very rare cases where a certain crimson red appears. In view of this tendency to wash off, the band of lettering was not cleaned.

Other Harwood *retablos* have been retouched with commercial water colors, apparently during the time when they were a part of the Mabel Dodge Luhan Collection.

9. THE ORIENTAL PAINTER, 1835-50

This folk artist has also been isolated and named by Boyd, the elliptic oriental eyes of his personages being one of the most prominent features of his workmanship. Of the dozen panel painters whose style has been definitely identified, the Oriental Painter is the least skilled in drawing anatomical lines. This is especially noticeable in the hands, which have all the appearance of rough dovetailing when in the folded position. That he tried hard to be realistic is indicated by the thumbs, which sometimes stand straight up behind entwined fingers, as on Harwood 11, another of the "missing" panels from that institution.

With all his shortcomings as a painter, the Oriental was one of the best (along with the Quill Pen Painter, *infra*) in the preparation of *yeso* surfaces and in grinding and preparing pigments. His colors are still clear, and the surfaces of his panels have withstood well the mischief of time and handling.

In addition to the characteristics mentioned, the *retablos* of the Oriental Painter show raiment and draperies in solid colors, with very little, if any, detail. Examples: Berg Collection, *Our Lady of Sorrows;*[28] Harwood 84, *Our Lady of Guadalupe;* Wells R-64, *Pieta* (Pl. 24).

10. THE DOT-DASH PAINTER, 1835-50

Working during the years just preceding and following American occupation, and in an unknown locality, there lived a painter who, because of the dignity of his figures and the frankness, simplicity and cleanness of his style, is one of the most charming of all New Mexican folk painters. His boards are all hand-adzed. His panels may be identified very often by the roughly brushed dots or dashes in various colors with which he decorated corners, borders and other unoccupied areas. This characteristic may be observed on Harwood 30, *St. Jerome* (where the lion has been completely scraped off), and on Harwood 43, *St. Augustine.* On the first mentioned panel the dots are red and the dashes black. The same arrangement of colors appears on his representation of St. Joseph, Barton 14.[29] He generally left his personages to speak for themselves, there being little decoration to distract the observer, and where there is decoration, large, empty spaces are present—Wells R-83, *St. Ignatius* (Pl. 25) and McCormick Bfmc nb6-87, both very much alike. All facial details are well-drawn, with straight, Greek noses, clearly outlined eyes and carefully drawn lips. His hands are always delicate, graceful, and well-proportioned.

Besides the St. Joseph panel mentioned, the Barton Collection has two other precious examples of the Dot-Dash Painter's work: No. 15, *Veronica's Veil,* and 16, *St. John*

Nepomucene. On the last-mentioned panel the crucifix held by the saint is one of the most delicate and realistic of any seen on New Mexican *retablos.*[30] Harwood 72, *St. John Nepomucene,* and Fiske Day R-34, *St. Rosalia of Palermo,* are also typical. Harwood 6, *St. Raymond Nonnatus* (Pl. 26), represents the Dot-Dash Painter at his best.

11. THE QUILL PEN PAINTER, 1835-55

The name applied by Boyd to this painter, whom she isolated, issues from the fact that more often than not he used a hard instrument, apparently a quill pen, to draw the finer lines and smaller details of his panels. This technique is particularly noticeable in the rendition of hands and facial details. The noses of his figures are usually very straight and angular, and the lower eyelid is indicated either by delicate shading or by a line much lighter and finer than that used to draw the upper lid.

One of the Quill Pen Painter's best panels is that representing the Trinity (Pl. 27). Another is Spanish Colonial Arts Society No. L.5.52-49, inscribed EL STO. ECC [sic] HOMO, where the artist employs eight different Passion symbols. Fiske Day No. 11 shows a young queen holding a Cross, which is identified as St. Isabel of Portugal. Carroll Sr-702, *St. Vincent Ferrer;* Wells R-40, *St. Christopher;* and *Christ Carrying His Cross,* Fiske Day R-24, are representative of the Quill Pen Painter's more folkish manner. Wells R-65, *Our Lady of the Rosary* (Pl. 28), has the symbols and attributes of both this advocation and of *Our Lady Queen of Heaven.* This *retablo* is distinctive in that the carved shell at the top is one of the most skillfully done in all New Mexican folk art. Barton 20 is a representation of St. Gabriel, or so it is intended to be,[31] judging from Evans No. A-110 which shows the three Archangels, Raphael, Michael and Gabriel. On the Barton panel

---

28. Repro. in SSM, Fig. 4.
29. Reproduced in ABC, No. 14.
30. Both Barton panels repro. in ABC, Nos. 15 and 16.
31. Repro. in ABC, No. 20.

Gabriel holds a monstrance, and on the Evans *retablo* he holds a chalice. Neither of these objects is proper to Gabriel, although the Lily in one case and the staff in the other are appropriate. It seems that the Quill Pen Painter is confused in his representation of Gabriel on the Evans panel, and that the Barton *retablo* may have been intended to represent the archangel Chamael, whose symbols are a staff and a chalice or monstrance. If this is so, we may add another saint to the sixty-three already identified in New Mexican folk art. The Quill Pen Painter did paint several saints quite uncommon in *santero* art, namely, St. Gabriel, St. Vincent Ferrer, St. Isabel of Portugal.

12. THE FLORAL PAINTER, 1850–70

The latest painter to be isolated by Boyd she has named the Floral Painter, because of his penchant for drawing floral and leafy de-signs and decorations on any portion of his *retablos*. He is very representative of the degeneration of folk painting as the nineteenth century wore on, for his drawing is most elementary, indicating little talent and great effort. Eyes are done in simple outline, with a dot anywhere within the outline, and hands are indefinable. An image of Our Lady holding the Christ Child, with both holding flowers, No. L.3.51-6 of the Museum of New Mexico Collection, reflects all of the features mentioned, as does also the representation of St. Acacius shown in Pl. 29. The Acacius panel is one of the few showing a well-drawn horse in all *santero* art. Astride the beast is a figure which has all the characteristics of New Mexican folk representations of St. James the Greater. In Hispanic history Santiago appeared everywhere, so there should be no objection to his showing up at the martyrdom of Acacius and his ten thousand companions.

7. BULTO CARVERS

ANY NUMBER of *bultos* are found with the name of the saint inscribed thereon, those bearing a date are the rare exception, and not a single image in the round has been discovered bearing the name of the artist. A representation of Our Lady of Refuge in the Taylor Museum is dated 1820,[1] and an image of St. Joseph in the Fred Harvey Collection, Albuquerque, bears the date 1828.

The task of identifying the individual carvers and painters of *bultos* has only started, for, as in the case of *retablos,* the investigator is obliged to tread upon undocumented ground. With *retablos* we have many inscriptions and two names, and with *bultos* we have but a handful of dates and four names, only two of which can be taken seriously with the information at hand. Under these circumstances Wilder has followed a line of thought previously entertained by the few students of New Mexican religious folk art and centered his efforts upon the classification of certain large groups of *bultos* according to area of geographic origin, coupled with stylistic features. The classification of *bultos* according to this plan may provoke some objection. It may be said, for example, that the styles attributed to given areas are found throughout northern New Mexico and southern Colorado, and in the case of some types as far south as Socorro, and consequently cannot be said to have been produced in a single, restricted region. However, there is a definite concentration of certain types and styles in limited areas, and as one departs from these districts the types concentrated there become less common. It would seem logical, therefore, to return to the area of heavier concentration and consider it as that of origin.

One of the obstacles in the way of identifying the authorship of *bultos* is that they were made by so many *santeros*. So far it has been possible to associate only one man with definite works. In all other cases the investigator must accept with qualification the memories of people who did not have personal knowledge of the *santeros* or their works.

Because of the fragility of the smaller parts and features of images in the round, these have suffered all sorts of mutilation, damage, and defacement. This by itself would be disturbing enough, but when we add to it the poor efforts of restoration by private owners and curio dealers the difficulties of identification are often increased. Heads, limbs, symbols and attributes have been supplied so inexpertly and erroneously in many cases that original appearances and character have been considerably altered. Repainting, sometimes with ordinary housepaint, is, to the lover of New Mexican *santos,* most annoying.

New Mexican *bultos* will be considered under the following divisions: A. Five Groups Classified According to Geographic Origin, B. The Gothic Group, C. Four Carvers Known by Name, D., A Name Without Works, E. *Bulto*-Making in the San Luis Valley.

---

1. Repro. in RFA, Pl. 43.

74 *saints in the valleys*

A. FIVE GROUPS CLASSIFIED ACCORDING TO GEOGRAPHIC ORIGIN

1. THE SANTA CRUZ VALLEY GROUP, 1775–1880

The Santa Cruz Valley, which took its name from the second oldest town in New Mexico, established by Vargas in 1695, straddles the line between Santa Fe and Rio Arriba counties. The early date established for the beginnings of this group of *bulto*-makers is predicated on information contained in the inventory of Domínguez in 1776 and that taken by Father Rosete in 1796, both at Santa Cruz. From all the evidence which it has been possible to assemble, it seems that New Mexican folk art of a religious character started in the village of Santa Cruz, passing almost immediately to the nearby villages of Córdova, Chimayó, Trampas, Chamisal, Ranchos de Taos, Taos, Abiquiú, El Rito, and gradually getting into almost any village of northern New Mexico.

The churches, chapels, and homes of both the Upper and Lower Santa Cruz valleys display *bultos* whose distinguished character places them in a superior category. They are not by any means the product of a single craftsman, but represent the work of a great number of *santeros* of similar stylistic leanings but who vary considerably in interpretive powers and technical skills. The Santa Cruz Valley Group, along with the work of Antonio Silva, Eusebio Córdova, and the authors of the Arroyo Hondo, the Gothic and the Tomé Area figures, all to be considered later, comes closest to achieving that sophistication and realism so characteristic of Spanish and Mexican baroque statuary. The only factors which kept the *bulto*-makers of these groups from absolutely attaining the attractiveness of academic art in their work were the lack of refined tools and materials and just a modicum of instruction. For untutored craftsmen, their work is extraordinary.

The realism of Santa Cruz *bultos* extends to all anatomical features, with carving and painting executed with taste, color, and competence. There are two distinctive types within the Santa Cruz Valley Group.[2] The principal type, and most numerous, is characterized by a tall, slightly leaning and graceful figure, with slightly protruding lips and eyeballs. This type is well exemplified by the four images illustrated in Pls. 31, 32, 33, and 34. The Wells Collection has four outstanding examples: B-37, *St. Isidore the Husbandman; St. Anthony of Padua; St. Roch;* and the *Christ Child.*[3] The Taylor Museum has any number of them, the following being exceptionally fine: *St. John the Baptist; St. Anthony of Padua; St. Francis Xavier; Our Lady of Sorrows; Our Lady of the Rosary* (two representations); *St. Rita of Cascia;* and the *Christ Child.*[4] The famous equestrian figure of *Santiago,* now restored and in a glass case, is another outstanding example of a Santa Cruz Valley *bulto,* and may be seen in the *Santuario* at Chimayó, its old and original home.[5]

2. THE TAOS GROUP, 1790–1875

The one characteristic common to the principal types of images in the round of the Taos Group, especially those representing Christ, is their great size, being considerably larger than representations from other areas with the sole exception of the Tomé Area Group, *infra.* In order to separate *bultos* of distinct inspiration, the Taos Group is subdivided into two classes.

a. *Penitente* images of Christ:

So-called *penitente bultos* may be found in almost any rural chapel, *morada* (chapter house), or collection of north-central New Mexico and southern Colorado. The name "*penitente* image" does not mean that they were necessarily made by members of the brotherhood of flagellants, as too many popu-

2. The second type will be considered under Eusebio Córdova, *infra.*
3. Last three repro. in SSM, Figs. 15, 20, and 16.
4. All repro. in RFA, Pls. 22, 2, 10, 12, 38, 48, 13, and 54.
5. *See* Boyd, "Señor Santiago de Chimayo," EP, 63, 3 (March, 1956), 69–72. The image of *Santiago* is reproduced on the cover of this issue.

lar writers have stated. Considering that the great years of New Mexican folk art were those when the *penitentes* flourished, the chances are that very few northern New Mexican men did not belong to the brotherhood. The name derives from the manner in which the images of Christ of this type reflect the bloody character of *penitente* practices.

The extravagant naturalism of the *Cristos* of this group sets them apart from any other class of New Mexican *bultos*. The arms, legs and head are often articulated so that they could be used for the re-enactment of the various scenes of the Passion. These *bultos* may be further identified by the extensive use of *yeso*-coated cloth, mica-encrusted eyes, and beards of modeled or sculptured *yeso*. The larger figures usually have wigs of human hair, either black, blond, or red. An excellent example of the use of cloth for the articulation of the joints is a *bulto* of the Gilberto Espinosa Collection shown in Pl. 35. The Man of Sorrows was a favorite *penitente* representation, and is the one most popular with the editors of art magazines,[6] but from a devotional point of view they are generally quite uninspiring, being among the most aesthetically unattractive of all New Mexican sacred images.

However, in the hands of an inspired and talented carver some of these *penitente* images of Christ are the equal of any representations of Christ Crucified anywhere. The new church of Santo Tomás at Abiquiú has retained only one of the many old *santos* which once graced the original chapel. These were removed to one of the local *moradas* (whether the Republican or Democratic is not known) when the old church was torn down. The remaining figure is one of the two great representations of Christ Crucified by a New Mexican *santero*, along with the image hung on the wall of the south chapel in the Church of Cristo Rey in Santa Fe. Like a number of other Crucifixes of the Taos Group, the one at Abiquiú has an opening in the left side of the back through which a suspended heart may be seen. Prominent lacerations cover the body, the knees are deeply wounded, and the eyes are open. The

hands and feet, as well as other anatomical features, are expertly carved. All members are carved separately and gracefully joined. This image now hangs on the left wall nearest the entrance to the church. It deserves to be placed over the main altar in place of the pretty, factory-made plaster image which now occupies this position.

Penitente images of Christ are numerous. A few outstanding examples, in addition to the three already mentioned, are: Taylor Museum, *Christ Crucified,* and five representations of *The Man of Sorrows.*[7] Denver Art Museum, *Christ Crucified.*[8] Wells Collection, *The Man of Sorrows.*[9] Also of the *penitente* type is the representation of *Christ in the Sepulcher* in the Taylor Museum, made by Miguel Herrera, *infra,* of Arroyo Hondo.[10]

b. Large images other than those of Christ:

The *bultos* of this sub-group are almost limited to representations of either the Blessed Mother or St. Joseph, with only an occasional depiction of St. Anthony or some other saint. The Taylor Museum has three *bultos* belonging to this sub-group: *Our Lady of Sorrows, Our Lady of the Rosary,* and *St. Joseph.*[11] Other images of this type may be seen in the Denver Art Museum, the Museum of New Mexico, and in the Mrs. Neil B. Field Collection at the University of New Mexico.

3. THE ARROYO HONDO GROUP, 1840–70

About ten miles northwest of Taos, and in the fertile river bottoms of the Hondo Valley, is the tiny village of Arroyo Hondo, settled in 1823, about the time that New Mexican *santería* was in full flower. The Taylor Museum has three *bultos* secured from the

6. *See* cover of *Magazine of Art,* XXXIII (March, 1940); also *Holiday,* 11, 2 (February, 1952), 42.

7. Repro. in RFA, Pls. 23, 24 and 25, 34 and 35, 36, 37, and 52.

8. Repro. in Color Slide No. 30, Dr. Block's *Santos. Our Religious Folk Art.*

9. *See* n. 6, above.

10. Repro. in RFA, Pls. 26 and 27; also in NMS, 5.

11. Repro. in RFA, Pls. 4, 47, and 18.

private chapel of Juan Medina of Arroyo Hondo. Beyond question the work of the same craftsman, the peculiar characteristics of these images in the round justify Wilder's classification of them in a separate geographic group. These *bultos* are representations of St. Bonaventure (Pl. 38), St. Francis of Assisi, and St. Joseph.

The Arroyo Hondo figures may be identified by the heaviness of the body from the waist down, a feature which creates an impression of firmness. Beards are full and symmetrically drawn, and the nose is long, narrow and sharp. The mouth is slightly open. The distinct and emphatic delineation of facial details is unexcelled by any other type. The decoration of the habit of St. Bonaventure is the *santero's* effort to duplicate the *estofado*, or painted relievos on a gilt ground, of Mexican and Spanish statuary, a technique which, happily, is coming back into vogue throughout the Catholic world.

The Denver Art Museum has a representation of St. Francis of Assisi which is so much like the three images mentioned that it is classed with them.[12] It is not by the same artist as the Medina figures. The crescent-shaped eyes of this image are reminiscent of those done by the Oriental Painter of *retablos,* and constitute the major point of difference between the Denver image and those in the Taylor Museum. Wells *bulto* B-49 of *St. Joseph* (Pl. 37) is another Arroyo Hondo figure, and the equal of any of them.

4. THE TOMÉ AREA GROUP, 1800–50

Tomé is a village about twenty-five miles south of Albuquerque. Originally the hacienda of Tomé Domínguez, and referred to in the early records as Nuestra Señora de la Inmaculada Concepción de Tomé Domínguez, it was destroyed during the revolt of 1680 and resettled shortly after 1740. Clustered about are the villages of Valencia, Adelino, La Constancia, San Fernando, and Peralta. In and around Tomé there developed around the turn of the nineteenth century, on the heels of the work of Antonio Silva, *infra* and of the same development in the Upper Rio Grande

Valley, what can rightfully be termed an independent school of folk *bulto*-making. The statuary of this area, which is neither numerous nor widely distributed, is distinguished by its large size and by what Dickey happily calls its "facile" execution. Antonio Silva was from this district, but only those works not from his hand will be considered here.

The image of St. Raphael the Archangel shown in Pl. 39 is quite typical of Tomé Area *bultos* in two significant respects, namely, the impression of life and the attractive proportions of the body. The garments are carved out of the wood, which is not common in New Mexican religious folk art.

The Church of Nuestra Señora de los Dolores at Manzano, a village some twenty-three miles to the west by south of Tomé, has an image of its patroness slightly more than three feet tall. The face of this image is representative of the Tomé Area figures, inclined to the "fleshy" side. It also has the comeliness which is typical of Tomé Area *bultos* of the Virgin, and was made to be dressed, for the body from the hipline down is constructed of an armature of staves around which cloth has been glued and sewn.

The magnificent *Christ Crucified* in the Church of Cristo Rey in Santa Fe, taken to the capital by Archbishop Gerken in 1938 from the church at Valencia, is the masterpiece of Tomé Area images, and with the same representation in the Church of Santo Tomás at Abiquiú, is the outstanding rendition of the Divine Victim in all *santero* art, unsurpassed even by most crucifixes coming from the art of the schools for its interpretation of Calvary (Pl. 40).

In the church at Tomé there is a *bulto* of The Man of Sorrows. Some of the villagers recall that it was done by the same *santero* who executed the statue of St. Bonaventure in the home of Mrs. Francisco Padilla in Tomé.[13] Others remember having heard that

---

12. Repro. in RFA, Pl. 5.

13. The owner of this image has identified it as a representation of St. Francis of Assisi. This saint is rarely represented holding a book in academic art, and is never so depicted in New Mexican folk art.

the artist was from the nearby village of Ade-lino, and still others vaguely recall that the carver of both the images was a woman.

The *bultos* of the Tomé Area Group are not surpassed by any in all New Mexican folk art, and are equalled by few. It is regrettable that such outstanding folk craftsmanship has been so lightly investigated by competent students of *santería*. It is just as lamentable that the folklore of the Tomé district has been so confused and rumpled by vague recollection and wishful thinking that only a very small part of it can be accepted as of value.[14]

5. THE MORA GROUP, 1830–70

A very common and widely distributed type of *bulto* is one which quite often has a flat body. The front of the neck, especially on figures of Christ Crucified, is also often flat. These images are sometimes referred to erroneously as Flat Figures, assuming that they are all so carved.[15] On the basis of concentration, and of common opinion among owners of Mora figures, it is thought that they originated in the area around Mora, a town to the east of the Sangre de Cristo Range. Some of the flat images of this group were carved from milled lumber, such as 2 × 4's and 2 × 6's, which accounts for the flat bodies and the flaring skirts of the Blessed Mother, the Christ Child, and a few saints.

Mora *bultos* are second only to those from the Santa Cruz Valley in number, and because of this factor and the stereotyped character of these images, it would seem that they were put out by the same *santería* or group of *santerías*, but certainly under the influence, if not direct supervision, of one man. They can scarcely be the work of one *santero*.

The frontispiece illustrates a characteristic Mora figure of the flat type. The face incorporates angular forms, the hairline is clearly defined, the nose is triangular, and the arches deep-cut. The chin is usually small, and the eyes oversized and almond-shaped. The general aspect is one of severity. Hands are carved with short, blunted fingers. Beards are squarish, usually divided into three parts, clean-cut grooves separating the sides from a

goatee. The costumes of Mora images are generally painted in red and black, with trims done in blue and yellow. The skin tones of many images of Christ Crucified are yellowish. The biceps are pronounced, and are stretched far into the muscles of the forearm. The latter muscles are also exaggerated, and are symmetrically disposed on both sides. This interpretation of the anatomy of the arm is not exclusive to Mora figures, for there are any number of both classified and unclassified crucifixes with almost identical carving. In fact, the same treatment of the arm is common to late medieval representations of Christ Crucified in Europe. The design of the loincloth of the figure in the frontispiece is quite typical of the ornamentation on all Mora *bultos*. Generally speaking, Mora images are the least attractive of all New Mexican folk-made statuary.

The smallest collection of New Mexican religious folk art has at least one example of a Mora *bulto,* an indication of the many surviving examples. Suffice it to call attention to the following: Carroll SB-11 is a representation of Christ in the Sepulcher, and the fact that it was secured in Los Mogotes, Colorado, shows how widely distributed Mora figures are. The oxen and the plow with St. Isidore the Husbandman (Pl. 41) are later additions, but the figure of the saint and the angel accompanying him are typical of Mora workmanship. Other Mora *bultos* are: Meem Collection, *The Holy Child of Atocha.*[16] Boyd Collection, *Angel Holding a Chalice.*[17] Taylor Museum, *St. Acacius, St. Barbara, Our Lady of the Rosary,* and *The Holy Family.*[18]

---

14. *See* Ellis, "Santeros of Tome," *The New Mexico Quarterly,* XXIV, 3 (Autumn, 1954); also Ellis "Tomé and Father J. B. R.," *New Mexico Historical Review,* XXX, 2 (April, 1955), 89–114, and *Ibid.,* XXX, 3 (July, 1955), 195–220. *Also* Chávez, "Comments Concerning 'Tomé and Father J. B. R.'," *Ibid.,* XXXI, 1 (January, 1956), 68–74.

15. Charles Carroll held the view that the Mora *bultos* were the work of the *retablo* painter Miguel Aragón, now identified as José Rafael Aragón. This is an untenable opinion, and one which Boyd rightfully does not consider. *See* Carroll, "Miguel Aragon, A Great Santero," EP, L, 3 (March, 1934), 49–64; *also* Boyd, SSM, 47–49.

16. Repro. in SSM, Fig. 9.

17. Repro. in SSM, Fig. 10.

18. Repro. in RFA, Pls. 1, 7, 8, and 39.

The Kleijkamp and Monroe Collection and the Detroit Institute of Arts both have Mora representations of The Holy Family.

B. THE GOTHIC GROUP, 1830–60

This group of *bultos* was first isolated and named by Boyd.[19] They were executed in northern New Mexico, principally in the Santa Cruz Valley area. As a group they constitute the greatest achievement of the New Mexican *bulto* carvers. As the name implies, there is in the general appearance of Gothic figures the same conventional expressions which characterize the statuary executed in stone and wood during the early Gothic period in Europe (1150–1300). Late Gothic figures are more graceful and natural. Early Gothic images are more slender than in real life, and the same observation may be made regarding New Mexican *bultos* of the Gothic Group, which also have the grace and relaxation of the late Gothic.

As exemplified by the Crucifixion shown in Pl. 42, the New Mexican Gothic *bultos* manifest considerable attention to anatomical details. The heads and faces are especially handsome, and from a devotional point of view they are perhaps the most appealing of all *santero* representations. This opinion applies especially to depictions of Christ Crucified.

Besides the Crucifixion shown in Pl. 43, the Wells Collection has six Gothic figures: B-45, *The Holy Trinity;*[20] B-1, *Christ Crucified;*[21] B-42, *St. Joseph;* B-43, *St. Joseph;* B-9, *St. Barbara;* and B-23, *Ecce Homo* (in the half-round). The Taylor Museum has an excellent Christ Crucified of the Gothic type,[22] as does also the Gilberto Espinosa Collection (in addition to the one shown in Pl. 42).

C. FOUR CARVERS KNOWN BY NAME AND WORKS

1. ANTONIO SILVA OF ADELINO AND VALENCIA, 17?–18?

We have in Antonio Silva an apparently legitimate *santero,* but a nebulous personality.

It has been intimated that his country of origin was Portugal, which is just as fanciful as his supposed training in art in either Portugal or Spain.[23] These erratic opinions and others of a similar character conspire to discount most of what is said about him. If Silva had studied art in Europe, and was a native of Portugal, he would be neither a New Mexican nor a *santero.* Judging on the basis of New Mexican history and the character of his work, Antonio Silva was in all probability just a good old New Mexican *santero* doing the best he could.

If we may place any credence in the identification of his name with the *bultos* credited to him, Antonio Silva is the earliest *bulto*-carver known by name, and one of the very best. It is said that in 1790, shortly after settling in Adelino, he started work on the crucifix which until recently hung over the main altar in the church at Tomé. (Pl. 44.) This figure is an excellent example of New Mexican *santero* art, done with the same materials and methods as the *bultos* of the Upper Rio Grande Valley. Also in 1790, Silva is said to have begun work on the five-foot *bulto* of *Our Lady of the Immaculate Conception* in the Tomé church.[24] The face of this Virgin is just as realistic and comely as any of the Santa Cruz Valley representations of Mary. Unfortunately, we have here another case of repainting, which, as usual, probably does not do justice to the original. Both the *Christ Crucified* and the *Virgin* by Silva are among the best *bultos* done by New Mexican folk artists.

The eleven oil paintings in the Tomé church have been attributed to Silva by his descendants and the villagers of that place. These canvases are late eighteenth century importations from Mexico, and the fact that they have been assigned to a New Mexican

---

19. *See* SSM, 65.

20. Repro. in SSM, Fig. 18.

21. Repro. in Macmillan, *Fifteen New Mexico Santos,* Pl. 3.

22. Repro. in RFA, Pls. 50 and 51.

23. For the background of Antonio Silva and *bulto*-making in the Tomé area see: Ellis, "Tomé and Father J. B. R.," and Chávez, "Comments Concerning 'Tomé and Father J. B. R.'" previously cited.

24. Repro. in Ellis, "Santeros of Tomé," *op. cit.*

santero is an indication of the amount of credence that can be placed in the information secured by Ellis in other matters related to him. What is needed in the case of Antonio Silva is just a modicum of documentation.

2. EUSEBIO CÓRDOVA OF CÓRDOVA, 1820?–80?

Within the Santa Cruz Valley Group of *bultos* there exists a type which has been called "the Córdova type." Some, if not all of these images are probably the work of one Eusebio Córdova, who, according to old residents of the village of Córdova, consulted some thirty years ago, fashioned *bultos* "a long time ago."[25] The Church of San Antonio at Córdova enshrines a statue of St. Peter which may be taken as typical of the images carved in that place. As usual, with all New Mexican *bultos,* the body is not especially well done, but the visage of the saint is as realistic as any in sophisticated art. Many *bultos* of the Santa Cruz Valley Group are of the Córdova type. From a point of view of academic realism and as an inspiration to devotion the Córdova type, along with the general Santa Cruz Valley Group, the Gothic images and the work of Antonio Silva, are the most pleasing and satisfying. All *santeros* were mindful of the representative content of their art and strove up to the limits of their skills for an effect that would bring aesthetic enjoyment.

An examination of the *bultos* of the groups and types mentioned will show that they are as attractive in form as any Christian images, and constitute a direct contradiction to the widespread notion that New Mexican *santos* are ugly. This view has been disseminated by popular magazines whose editors seem to choose the homeliest, crudest and most "dramatic" *bultos* and *retablos* to illustrate their articles. The idea seems to be that if an image is attractive and realistic it cannot be representative of folk craftsmanship.

Plate 45, representing St. Isidore the Husbandman, is a good example of Eusebio Córdova's work, and is much like the St. Peter mentioned above, as is also a *bulto* of the Wells Collection depicting St. Joseph.

3. MIGUEL HERRERA OF ARROYO HONDO, 1850?–18?

There is not much to say about this *bulto*-maker except that the old residents of Arroyo Hondo informed Wilder in 1943 that the exceptional representation of Christ in the Sepulcher in the Taylor Museum was carved by him. The image is in the style and manner of the Taos *penitente bultos,* which is easily explained by the proximity of Arroyo Hondo to Taos. It is articulated at the shoulders, and the jaw is articulated, the latter controlled by a string.

4. JUAN RAMÓN VELÁZQUEZ OF CANJILÓN, 1865–99

Canjilón is a village in Rio Arriba County with a population of about seven hundred persons and is the trading center of a small area. Mr. Elmer Shupe of Taos is the discoverer of the *bulto*-maker Velázquez. The substance of Mr. Shupe's letter[27] relates the manner in which he established the identity of this *santero:*

In 1899, when he was nine years of age, Mr. Shupe was living with his family in Canjilón. The family knew a Mr. Velázquez and his son Pablo, but did not know that the elder Velázquez was a *santero.* In 1943, while living at La Madera in the employ of the Forestry Service with a crew of forty men from the nearby villages of El Rito, Vallecitos, Petaca and Las Tablas, he asked these men if they owned any old *santos.* He was introduced to one Adolfo Ortega, the *hermano mayor,* or head of the *penitentes,* at La Madera, who sold the *santos* of the *morada* to him. Among the *bultos* acquired was a representation of The Man of Sorrows, and at a glance Mr. Shupe recognized that it was made by the same *santero* who had fashioned the image of The Man of Sorrows in the Taylor Museum,[28] and which he had bought at Plaza

---

25. *See* SSM, p. 64.
26. *See* Wilder, *New Mexican Santos,* p. 5. The image is reproduced in this reprint, and also in RFA, Pls. 26 and 27.
27. *Letter* dated October 4, 1952.
28. Repro. in RFA, Pl. 52.

Sevilleta in 1928. He asked Mr. Ortega for the name of the artist and was told that it was Juan Ramón Velázquez of Canjilón. Mr. Shupe then informed Mr. Ortega that he had known a Pablo Velázquez and his father in Canjilón, and Mr. Ortega stated that Pablo's father was Juan Ramón, the *santero*. Mr. Ortega was about seventy-seven years of age in 1943 when Mr. Shupe contacted him, so he was born about 1866, and therefore grew up during Juan Ramón Velázquez' active years.

Mr. Cresencio Montoya, also of La Madera, supported Mr. Ortega's information. The identity of our *bulto*-carver is further established by another experience of Mr. Shupe. In 1944 he bought a third *bulto* of The Man of Sorrows at Casita, from a Miss Romero, who was about sixty years of age. This image was almost a duplicate of his two previous purchases. Miss Romero told him that Juan Ramón Velázquez had made it. Further, Mr. Shupe worked with one Janero Madril of Cebolla and Canjilón for four years, and this man stated that as a youngster he had known Juan Ramón Velázquez as a *santero*.

As may be determined by comparing the representation of Christ Crucified of Pl. 46 with any other New Mexican image in the round, Velázquez' *bultos* are easy to identify. The eyes are always large, and, with the exception of crucifixes, open, with deep-cut upper lids and heavily outlined details. Eyebrows are unusually wide and sweeping. The forehead bulges, with a deep cut at the point where it is joined to the bridge of the nose. The nose is long, with deep furrows separating it from the cheeks, which are concave in the area in line with the mouth. The mouth is always small and half-puckered. If any other characteristic were necessary to identify the work of this *santero,* the form of the ear alone would suffice, for it is divided into two ellipsoid parts, unlike that of any other carver. All anatomical features other than those mentioned are rather formless. Up to about 1880 Velázquez made and used his own tempera colors; after this date he used common house paint.[29]

Besides that of The Man of Sorrows, the Taylor Museum has a *bulto* of St. Raphael by Velázquez.[30] Other known *bultos* by him are: *An armless Virgin,* No. 2.34-1335 of the Museum of New Mexico; *St. Michael,* the property of Ann Parish (Mrs. Josiah Titzel) of Georgetown, Conn.; *Christ Crucified,* No. 50 of the Kleijkamp and Monroe Collection; and a precious *angelito* in the collection of Dr. T. M. Pearce of Albuquerque.

D. A NAME WITHOUT WORKS

TOMÁS SALAZAR
OF TAOS, 1813–70's?

The village of Los Valdeses is about six miles from the town of Del Norte, in the San Luis Valley of southern Colorado. The *penitentes* used to flourish in this area, and if we can place any credence in the following account, the *morada* at Los Valdeses contained at one time a quantity of *bultos* said to be the handiwork of one Tomás Salazar of Taos. Mr. Gavino Valdés, a native of Los Valdeses, was residing in Santa Fe in 1938 when, in his seventy-eighth year, he acted as informant to Miss Carmen Espinosa. Don Gavino related how, when he was a boy of eight or nine (1868–69) he used to go to the marshes near Los Valdeses with the son of Tomás Salazar, Florencio, to gather old seasoned wood for image-making purposes. He further related that they would gather chicken feathers, wrapping several together with thread, leaving only the tips exposed, for use as brushes. He judged that Tomás Salazar was about fifty-five years of age at that time, which would establish the 1860's as the period of his supposed image-making career, and 1813 or 1814 as the date of his birth.

29. *See* Espinosa, "The Discovery of the *Bulto*-Maker Ramón Velázquez of Canjilón," EP, 61, 6 (June, 1954), 185–90; *also* Boyd, "Addendum to Paper on José E. Espinosa's Ramon Velazquez," *Ibid.*, 190–91.
30. Repro. in RFA, Pls. 15 and 16.

E. BULTO-MAKING
IN THE SAN LUIS VALLEY

Beginning in the middle of the nineteenth century, a goodly number of New Mexicans, principally from Taos and Rio Arriba counties, migrated to the fertile San Luis Valley in south-central Colorado. Although we may be certain that there were *santeros* in this area, no information concerning them has been found in which we may place any confidence, coming to us as it does from the most uncertain oral tradition and unsupported by any examples of workmanship. William L. Wallrich, in an article titled "The Santero Tradition in the San Luis Valley," mentions three supposed *santeros* by name:[31] Antonio Herrera of Taos, who was established in San Acacio, just west of San Luis, in 1872, and who died between 1890 and 1900; Francisco Vigil of San Luis, about whom only the name is offered; and Juan Ascedro Maes of San Luis, who was still living in 1949, a half-century after the last *santero* was at rest!

As the art of image-making in New Mexico was still in its prime in 1850, when the migrations to the San Luis Valley started, it may be reasonably assumed that the craft of painting and carving sacred images was part of the baggage carried along with other folk practices. Most of the images found today in the San Luis Valley are of the Santa Cruz Valley and Taos groups. Carroll *bulto* SB-1049, representing The Man of Sorrows, was secured in the San Luis Valley. The heaviness of the lower part of the body is very remindful of the Arroyo Hondo figures. The face of this image is streaked with blood, which explains the identification, but the habit and the disposition of the hands indicate that it was originally either a St. Anthony or a St. Joseph. Carroll *bulto* SB-11, a Mora Valley representation of Christ in the Sepulcher, was secured in Los Mogotes, Colorado.

Bultos found in the San Luis Valley which are unique in style, or which resemble New Mexican types in only some respect, may very possibly be the work of local craftsmen, but up to the present time nothing whatever is known about them. There is a late type of *bulto* with glass eyes which is occasionally found in southern Colorado. The eyes were secured from large dolls, which became plentiful toward the end of the nineteenth century.

The fact that New Mexican types of *bultos* predominate in southern Colorado is evidence enough that New Mexican *santeros* visited this area.

---

31. *See* Bibliography.

82

8. the saints & their images in new mexican life

THE ONE great cultural force in Spain since the years of persecution under Diocletian, and throughout the Spanish-Colonial empire since the days of discovery, conquest and colonization, was the Catholic Church. The traditional beliefs, practices and devotions of the Church were as much a part of the daily existence of the Hispanic peoples as was retiring at night to bring needed rest to weary bones. These factors nurtured the spirit of religion and fostered the desire for sacred images in New Mexico.

Spain and her colonies escaped the worst abuses of the Renaissance, and they did not suffer the upheavals experienced by the remainder of Europe during the time of the Protestant Revolt and the eighteenth-century social, political and philosophical revolutions. "The agencies that grew out of the Reformation fell on the vast body of Christian art that inconceivably glorified all Western Europe at the end of the fifteenth century. . . . Outside Italy and Spain little escaped, compared with what had once been. . . . It was ruin and extinction worse even than that of the Iconoclasts of a thousand years before in the Byzantine Empire."[1] Neither the Revolt nor the revolutions of the eighteenth century had very much effect beyond the Pyrenees, and Catholic practices remained intact among the Spanish people. The reverence of the Spaniard for Christian sacred images was carried over to America by the conquistadores and colonists, quite as instinctively as they and the missionaries brought with them the tenets of

a faith which their ancestors had practiced for fifteen centuries.

The religious practices of a people can be appraised only through a knowledge of their history and an appreciation of the ambient in which they lived. In order to look with sympathy and understanding upon the veneration of sacred images in colonial New Mexico we must realize that the people of that time and place were frontiersmen, with all the moral virtues and weaknesses, all the practical gifts and intellectual shortcomings of any group living on the fringes of civilization. Unlearned, in the main, they were separated from an intellectual understanding of Catholicism by barriers of philosophy and theology. Although they drew close to the saints, the line drawn by theology between the worship due God and the veneration due the saints was never erased by them. Every traditional prayer, every traditional song, speaks and sings eloquently of this fact. The veneration of sacred images in colonial New Mexico, lacking all affectation, was the comfort and refuge of a brave and pious people whose daily life was an unending struggle to secure a lean and meager subsistence from a stingy soil, who were constantly exposed to insecurity and danger, and who were left with little help from and often ignored by a distant governmental authority.

In New Mexico, as in all Catholic regions since the victory of the West in the iconoclastic

---

1. Cram, *The Catholic Church and Art,* p. 95.

controversies, sacred images have ever played an important part in the lives of the people. Whether the house of a man of substance or the adobe shelter of a sheepherder, no New Mexican home was without its sacred images. To this day an image of the patron saint, of Christ, or of the Virgin Mother, and usually of all three, reposes in the homes, chapels, churches and even the business establishments of Spanish-speaking communities. It may be the image of the saint whose name is borne by the head of the household or by a member of the family, or perhaps the saint who, for some good reason, has been chosen as the protector of the home or ranch. The locality may have been reached on the feast day of the saint, or the building of the home started or completed on that day. Again, the granting of a petition may have prompted the adoption of a certain saint, Christian title, or Marian advocation as patron.

Throughout the colonial period, whenever the Spaniard established a settlement he invariably placed it under the protection of one of the saints. Ground was broken for a place of worship almost simultaneously with the placing of a roof over his head, and this church or chapel was always dedicated and a patron immediately selected to look after the spiritual and material welfare of the new community. In New Mexico and adjacent territory to the north, that is, the southern part of Colorado, as elsewhere throughout the world wherever the Spaniard has trod, "every landmark, stream and mountain range of importance honored Spanish saint or deity, long before Pike began his dubious wanderings. . . ."[2] It was an "almost invariable custom to seek Heaven's blessings on their discoveries by naming them for the Persons of the Trinity or the favorite titles of the Blessed Mother, or the saint or feast day, or some suggested scriptural or spiritual association. In fact, from the names they assigned to the capes, rivers, missions, towns, and forts . . . could be compiled the Litany of the Saints and an almost complete calendar of the ecclesiastical year."[3] Merely as a side task while reading New Mexican history it was possible to com-

pile a list of 95 different names applied to 310 different landmarks, missions, or settlements, 163 of which remain to this day. Their distribution is as follows: Saints: 62; Marian titles: 54; Christian titles: 37; General: 10.

From the time of the expeditions into New Mexico of the last twenty years of the sixteenth century to a time beyond the days of American occupation, by far the greatest number of rivers, streams, springs, pools, lakes, mountains, ranges, peaks, hills, valleys, plains, passes, canyons, land tracts, land grants, haciendas, ranches, towns, villages, settlements, military camps, mines, and, of course, missions, honored a saint, a feast day, a sacred object, event or association. More, perhaps, than any other convention, this traditional custom demonstrates the religious spirit of the Spanish explorers and colonists.

In most cases the geographic name is the key to the date upon which it was applied, for often a place or landmark was given the appellation of the saint or the name of the feast on whose day it was reached or observed. In the days of exploration and expansion, names were applied while an expedition was on the march. This accounts for the existence of cases where the same landmark or locality was named two and even three times, now by one expedition, now by another. Because these expeditions were not organized for purposes of settlement, few of the names bestowed during their course have survived. Only during the seventeenth and eighteenth centuries, when areas or localities were settled and frequented, were place names more apt to become permanent.

Many of the names of the older settlements were originally very long, but the passing of time and the dictates of practicality have reduced them to their shortest form, and, excepting a few cases, the sacred part of the name has been dropped. Santa Fe, the second oldest city in the United States, was first named La Villa Real de Santa Fe; Santa Cruz was originally called La Villa Nueva de Santa Cruz de los Españoles Mexicanos del Rey

---

2. Thomas, *After Coronado*, p. 1.

3. Kenny, *The Romance of the Floridas*, pp. 24-25.

Nuestro Señor Don Carlos Segundo, the first and last time this overburdened title was ever used; the village of Tomé was named Nuestra Señora de la Concepción de Tomé Domín-guez; and Albuquerque was first named La Villa de San Francisco Xavier de Alburquer-que, changed in April, 1777, to La Villa de San Felipe de Neri de Alburquerque.

It was to the patron saint of the home, the ranch, the village, or the town that the indi-vidual, the family, or the community offered special prayers and made petitions for relief from sickness or tribulation, for the blessing of crops, or for protection from the many dangers to which an agricultural and pastoral people living on the outposts of civilization were constantly exposed. Whenever sickness visited a member of the household, an image of a saint was placed in the sickroom and the help of the prototype implored. Images were often carried from the church to the home, a candle or lantern held before them and accom-panied by the singing of hymns by the proces-sion of friends and relatives. The heavy days of mourning following a death were lightened and made bearable by visits to the image, the faith of the people never suffering because of previous failure to elicit the intercession of the saint whose help was sought.

Whenever a special favor was to be re-quested, or perhaps in fulfillment of a promise, the image of a saint was set up in the principal room of the house and neighbors and friends were invited to a night of prayer. This is called *velorio de santo,* night watch for a saint. The element of diversion was not lacking, for at midnight refreshments were served.

It was not unusual for an image to enjoy a singular reputation, its prototype dispensing favors liberally. In such a case the *santo* was always traveling, taken from home to home and even from village to village, borrowed by friend and foe, neighbor and stranger.

In periods of drought the image of the patron of the village or district was carried through the fields, as has been the custom for centuries in all Catholic areas of the world. In New Mexico it was and is the images of St. Isidore the Husbandman and Our Lady of Guadalupe. This custom has been narrated in countless stories and novels since medieval times. Also in New Mexico as elsewhere, this practice has produced a rosary of traditional tales, some borrowed from other Hispanic areas, others developing almost similarly due to the nature of human reactions to supernat-ural phenomena.

Fragments of images were sometimes re-moved and thrown into a field as an offering for an abundant harvest, or parts of an image were burned and the ashes used for the same purpose. Pieces of *santos* were also burned to secure ashes for Ash Wednesday, or to be used as relics are used. When an image was broken or damaged beyond repair it was com-pletely burned and the ashes gathered for the purposes mentioned.

The myriad problems incident to the rug-ged life of farmers, sheepmen, cattlemen, and horsemen, in short, the daily concerns of peo-ple living close to Mother Earth, called for special patrons from the long list of holy men and women whose own lives reflected a special interest in or association with specific situa-tions.[4] With few exceptions, the invocations and patronage practiced and selected in New Mexico are common among Catholic peoples everywhere. The fact that many of these prac-tices are based upon fanciful and sometimes even ridiculous legends should not disturb the most learned and sophisticated, for docu-mented biographies of saints who lived in modern times present materials more amazing than the popular mind could ever imagine.

Images of Christ and the Blessed Mother are still dressed in the finest handiwork of their devotees. The adornment of the Virgin extends beyond elaborate tunics, dresses, man-tles, petticoats, and shoes to the use of jewelry of every sort, such as rings, earrings, combs, bracelets, necklaces, diadems, halos, and crowns.[5] The most richly endowed in this re-

---

4. *See* Appendix B. III, Representations of the Saints With the Principal Invocations and Patronage in New Mexico.

5. In 1663 one Fray Alonso de Posadas pronounced cen-sures in the church in Santa Fe "because of some jewels which had been stolen from an image of the most holy

spect has always been Our Lady of Victory, *La Conquistadora,* in the cathedral in Santa Fe. The church inventories of 1796 list dozens upon dozens of the items mentioned. In the poorer New Mexican rural chapels the practice of adorning images is almost confined to the use of all sorts of worthless objects, but unquestionably just as acceptable as valuable offerings. In the *Santuario* at Chimayó, for example, some images are burdened with crocheted purses and dime-store trinkets, chains, and plastic stirring rods, often, the villagers say, the offerings of children who see beauty in anything colorful or strange. During August, 1950, the author found the little *bulto* of St. James the Greater at Chimayó astride a bronzy horse of the drugstore variety, the original charger hanging on a wall nearby. Hung around the neck of the patron of Spanish arms was a plastic motto of World War II which read, "Let's get it done."[6]

Ex votos in the form of little images of wood, cloth, or metal testify to the gratitude of those who have received divine favors. They are placed on or near a *bulto* or *retablo.*

The saints are not only rewarded but reprimanded. Fresh candles, new clothing or *ex votos* are supplied when the saints are invoked or thanked, but many are the poor *santos* who have spent lonely hours or days in the darkness of a chest, a storeroom, or a closet, or wrapped in a blanket, or turned toward the wall for failure to listen to the pleas of a devotee who felt that he deserved better treatment. In the cases of St. Joseph and St. Anthony, and even the Virgin Mother, a cruel punishment was resorted to when desperate measures seemed to be the only way out of an impasse, namely, the removal of the Christ Child from their arms.

The name Mary is probably given to more Catholic girls than any other, and New Mexican girls are no exception. For many generations the name has been used with specific advocations, resulting in such names as Maria del Carmen, de los Dolores, de la Merced, de la Soledad, de la Luz, de la Asunción, de la Concepción, del Rosario, de la Candelaria, de Guadalupe, del Pilar, de la Piedad, del

Refugio, de los Remedios, etc. Other Christian names are used in combination: Josefa de la Asunción, Juana de la Concepción. Many of the same titles were added to masculine names: Juan de los Dolores, Juan de los Reyes, Manuel de la Cruz, Antonio de Jesús, José de Jesús y María, etc. Toward the end of the eighteenth century the second part of the combination began to be applied alone, so that we find both men and women bearing such names as Dolores, Merced, Concepción, Jesús, Jesús María, Cruz, Reyes, Carmen, Rosario, Guadalupe, Refugio, Pilar, etc.[7]

Romances (popular ballads) and *coplas populares* (popular quatrains) of ancient Spanish origin are still recited to a galaxy of saints, to Christ, and to the Virgin Mother. They have been collected by the hundreds. *Alabados,* or hymns of praise of the Blessed Sacrament, the Virgin and the saints have also been collected in quantity. Some are of Spanish origin; others apparently are of New Mexican composition.[8]

The ceremonies of Holy Week have always been a major event in New Mexico. The enactment of the Passion of Our Lord was a common practice during the past century. Today scenes from the Passion are still presented by the *hermanos penitentes* in several villages of northern New Mexico and southern Colorado. The annual Passion Play at Tomé, some thirty miles south of Albuquerque, is done in the truest spirit of Spanish and New Mexican tradition, reflecting the piety and the dignity of the villagers in the practice of their faith. Old popular dramas based upon New Testament themes related to the feasts of Christmas and the Epiphany, all of Spanish origin,

Virgin, Our Lady, in the church of the pueblo of Nambé." Hackett, *Historical Documents,* III, 259.

6. This image has since been completely renovated and restored. *See* E. Boyd, "Señor Santiago de Chimayó," EP 63, 3 (March, 1956), 69–72.

7. *Maria* or *Mary* are not uncommon names for men in England, Portugal, France, Belgium, and Italy. *Jesus* is known among the Greeks.

8. *See* Aurelio M. Espinosa, "Romancero Nuevomejicano," *Revue Hispanique,* XXXIII (1915), 446–560; "New Mexican Spanish Folklore, Parts I-XI," *Journal of American Folklore,* Vols. 23–29. *See also* Juan B. Rael, *The New Mexican Alabado, passim.*

are also presented in the rural sections. *Las Posadas* (The Inns) relates in octosyllabic verse the Gospel story of the Virgin Mother and St. Joseph wandering through the streets of Bethlehem on Christmas night seeking shelter. *Los Pastores* (The Shepherds) dramatizes the birth of Christ and the adoration of the shepherds. *Los Reyes Magos* or *La primera persecución de Jesús* (The Three Wise Men or The First Persecution of Jesus) tells of the visit of the Magi and of the flight into Egypt. *El Niño Perdido* (The Lost Christ Child) recites in dramatic form the story of the Child Jesus in the temple.

In a land where the saints have brought so much solace to the people it naturally follows that the feasts of the saints have long been set aside as days for very special acts of devotion and manifestations of joy. Since the earliest days of the New Mexican colony, fiestas have constituted the principal events of the year in nearly every village, town, and city established by the Spanish.[9] The eve of the saint's day, or of some special advocation of Our Lord or His mother, echoes with the recitation of special prayers, in the home, the chapel, or the church. This is followed by the inevitable *fandango,* which, since the coming of the *americano,* is called a *baile.* On the feast day itself, religious ceremonies invariably initiate the festivities. Mass is celebrated, usually followed by a procession, and the remainder of the day is one of gaiety and companionship. Previous to and for some time after American occupation there were foot races, horse races, chicken pulls *(la corrida del gallo),* and other contests, followed in the evening by another dance, where to the music of guitars and violins *la cuna, la escoba, el paso doble, la varsoviana, la raspa,* and other regional dances were the order of the evening.

The principal feast days of the Church and of the saints are still often ushered in by the lighting of bonfires, *luminarias,* an ancient custom. "On that night, a rather stormy one," wrote Father Benavides in 1626, "they lighted their lumanarias, and celebrated as much as they could."[10]

Today, numerous villages, towns and cities throughout New Mexico celebrate their fiestas in much the same way as they have been celebrated since the days of empire. Santa Fe yearly celebrates the recapture of the capital by Vargas, which took place on December 30, 1693. This commemorative event was revived in 1712 by order of the governor, the Marquez de la Peñuela. One of the high points of the Santa Fe fiesta is the homage paid to *La Conquistadora,* who shares honors with the great *conquistador* who made it possible for the city to become once again the center of Spanish life in New Mexico. Every year, on the Sunday following Corpus Christi, the image of *La Conquistadora* is carried in procession from the cathedral to the chapel of *Nuestra Señora del Rosario* on the outskirts of Santa Fe. There the Virgin remains for eight days (formerly nine), during which time a novena is made in her honor.

In old Albuquerque, founded in 1706, annual festivities have taken place on May 26 since around 1777, about the time St. Philip Neri was adopted as patron. Following the celebration of Mass in the old church the image of the patron is carried in procession around the plaza. The market booths and *fandangos* of other days have been forgotten by the new generations, who have replaced them with dime dances and other attractions of our contemporary civilization, in much the same way that horse races and chicken pulls replaced the miracle plays and military games of early colonial times.

From the time of his arrival in 1851, Bishop Lamy encouraged the celebration of feast days and the holding of processions, both ancient Christian practices. Neither he nor his European-born associates, however, took the slightest interest in the religious art of the people, which, in the larger towns, was replaced with prints and conventional plaster

9. *See* Aurora Lucero White, "Folkways and Fiestas," *This is New Mexico,* Santa Fe, 1948, pp. 260–65. *Also,* Juan B. Rael, "New Mexican Spanish Fiestas," *California Folklore Quarterly,* I (January, 1942), 83. *Also,* Florence Hawley Ellis, "Passion Play in New Mexico," *New Mexico Quarterly,* XXII, 2 (Summer, 1952), 200–12.

10. Hodge, Hammond, Rey, *Fray Alonso de Benavides' Revised Memorial of 1634,* p. 128.

images. It is not a happy task to relate that the Spanish, Mexican, New Mexican and American clergy have all established a poor record with respect to the preservation of *santos,* those both homely and comely images so dear to the hearts of the people.

A story still fresh in the memories of the old folks around Santa Cruz gives an idea of the attachment of the people to their home-made religious images. This incident was related to the author by Father José Cubells who served in the parish of the Holy Cross for some years, and concerns the case of Father G. Hallterman, of Belgian ancestry, assigned to the parish in 1903. The records at Santa Cruz disclose that he served there until 1918. During his first year at Santa Cruz, Fr. Hallterman was so shocked by the appearance of a *santero* crucifix in the Corpus Christi procession that he exclaimed: *"¡Quítame de adelante este esperpento!"* "Remove this horrible thing from my presence!" Epilogue: Fr. Cubells showed the author the holes left by the shotgun pellets in one of the frames of the rectory door through which Fr. Hallterman made his escape from the angry *santacruceños.* While not necessarily approving of such violent measures, we can thank the spirit of the men of Santa Cruz for the fact that to this day their church is a treasure chest of old *santero* art, in spite of the yearly exodus of old pieces and the repainting of old church furniture, instigated by clergymen who have no regard whatever for the history and traditions of the people they serve.

Around 1900 the rural people of New Mexico began to dispose of their *santos,* bartering them away for a pittance along with pieces of old silver and other articles which might bring them a small return. However, it did not take them long to learn the value placed upon their *santos* by merchants and collectors, prices which have risen so that the struggling *paisano* can scarcely afford to keep his old *bultos* and *retablos.* There are still many images left in the homes of the people, and some old and little-used *moradas* are well stocked with them. Along with the spreading appreciation of *santos,* and as under all circumstances where material values are involved, none of the folk-made images displayed for veneration in the chapels and churches, or for public edification in institutional collections are safe from the sticky-fingered gentry. Recently these simulacra have had a not-so-strange way of disappearing from the unguarded rural sanctuaries. Even a large skin painting was taken some years ago from the walls of the Museum of New Mexico. Through fair means and foul, these sacred heirlooms are passing into alien hands, in many instances merely to decorate a niche in a New Mexican-style home whose master may be unable to identify the representation; in others to attract attention in the marts of commerce, where they are for sale alongside of contemporary fakes which could mislead only an absolute stranger.

If *santos* are collected, conditioned, and preserved by those who are alive to their historical, artistic, and spiritual significance, seeing in them more than the sometimes rough artistry which meets the unbelieving eye, it is gratifying to know that these discerning people are helping to preserve, with fitting care and reverence, the sweet relics of a great cultural and religious history.

The last of the old *santeros* long ago laid down the tools of his craft. There is no longer heard along the winding, narrow, and dusty streets and paths of New Mexican villages the thud of the adz, the swish of the knife, nor the soothing grind of volcanic stone. Neither are the passerby's nostrils greeted with the fragrance of hard-earned pigments, dyes, and adhesives issuing from the open doorway of the home or *santería.* But, so long as a single *bulto* or *retablo* survives the abrasives of time, the New Mexicans of colonial descent may gratefully recall the *santeros* of old who, impelled by their spiritual aspirations and with their ingenuity, resourcefulness and folk skills, helped man those bastions that have always guarded the precious heritage of faith.

appendixes

APPENDIX A

CHRISTIAN ICONOGRAPHY AND THE SANTERO

THE SAINTS are always depicted in art with two main classes of objects: *symbols* and *attributes*. The saints may be represented with one or the other class, or with both classes. *Symbols* refer to abstract qualities, such as learning, purity, piety, patience, fortitude, etc. *Attributes* represent objects related to personal histories or legends. To be called an attribute an object must be shown with the figure. Thus, the lily, when shown with the Blessed Mother, is her attribute, but when shown alone standing for her purity it is her symbol. When the lily stands alone as representative of the Virgin herself, it is her *emblem*. An emblem, therefore, is a kind of symbol, but represents the concrete instead of the abstract. There is a fourth group, which is also a species of the genus *symbol,* called a *type.* As an example, we may consider the story of the brazen serpent which, when looked upon, healed those in the desert under Moses who had been bitten by the fiery serpents (*Numbers* XXI). If only a mental picture of a brazen serpent is formed, without any association with the phenomenon of healing, it is a symbol; but if the brazen serpent is associated with salvation through Christ, it is a type. This complex aspect of Christian iconography is given only to make a relatively complete statement, since all four groups are found in New Mexican folk art. As it is difficult at times to distinguish between symbols and types on the one hand, and attributes and emblems on the other, the various objects shown with Christ, the Virgin, and the saints in New Mexican folk art will be considered only under the two principal genera *symbols* and *attributes*.

The use of symbols and attributes by artists from early Christian times to about 1300 was an exceedingly complicated practice. This statement is particularly true of symbols. During the period mentioned there were few portraits, in either painting or sculpture, as we know them. Artists executed conventional figures and used countless symbols and attributes for purposes of identification. The process of simplification started during the early Gothic period (1150–1300), when, due to the limited use of symbols and attributes, the artists often painted or carved the name of the saint in order to avoid any mistake in identification. After Giotto (1266?–1337) the symbols and attributes used in all previous periods were for the most part forgotten, and although artists of the Renaissance introduced new attributes for later saints, this aspect of sacred art was immeasurably simplified. As every other feature of the "new learning," this practice spread over the greater part of Europe, and forms the principal force behind the use of symbols and attributes down to the present day.

The need for some authority in Christian art is indicated by the publication in 1568 at Louvain of Molanus' *De sanctis Imaginibus et Picturis,* the first treatise on the subject. It is more than probable that this manual, excellent for its time, was at the disposal of the sculptors and painters of colonial Spanish America. Another volume which may have been available to them in later years is that of Padre Interián de Ayala, written originally in Latin but published in the Spanish translation of Luis de Durán *El Pintor christiano* [sic] *y erudito,* Madrid, 1782. Ayala drew extensively from Molanus.

It is well known that the iconography of painting and sculpture in Spanish America was but a continuation of European practices, especially as found on woodcuts and engravings of middle-European origin. These had found their composition in general European practice. We must also consider the influence of Spanish statuary and painting, brought into Spanish America by the first explorers and increasing in quantity as new areas were opened for settlement. The learned artists of Mexico were followed by their less sophisticated colleagues, the folk artists, and both of these directly influenced the *santeros* of New Mexico. Learned influences are found in woodcuts and engravings, either separate or in books of devotion, missals or breviaries, and in the paintings on canvas and buffalo hide, miniature paintings on wood, tin, copper and linen, and polychromed wooden statuary. The influence of Mexican popular religious art upon the *santero* was also great. An examination of Mexican popular votive paintings of the eighteenth and nineteenth centuries discloses the great similarity of their iconography to that of the handiwork of the New Mexican image-maker. For example, there are fifteen representations in New Mexican folk art done almost exactly as they appear in Mexican votive paintings used to illustrate a single volume.[1]

The saints popular in New Mexican tradition and folk art are for the most part the same ones which have enjoyed the special veneration of the faithful in every Christian age and clime. However, as with all Catholic peoples, the Spanish Colonials of New Mexico have been particularly devoted to certain saints and advocations having an endemic or representative association with their history. A study of the images found in the chapels, churches, convents, hospitals and public buildings of Mexico from the early days of Spanish settlement down to the present shows that the saints most honored there are the same ones widely venerated throughout the Spanish-speaking world, including New Mexico.

The use of symbols and attributes in New Mexican folk art is, therefore, very faithful to practice and tradition. In those cases where the identity of a saint is difficult or impossible to determine, and there are very few such cases, it is generally because of the absence of symbols and attributes rather than the incorrect use of them. In New Mexican folk art, as in the works of the masters, it is not always possible to identify an image by a single symbol or attribute, but a combination of two or more usually gives the necessary clues. Considering that the *santero* did not always use as many symbols and attributes as artists of academic tradition, the problems of identification are sometimes, but not often, bothersome. Also, there are few cases where the symbols and attributes employed in New Mexican folk art are based upon the whim or caprice of the *santero.* Even in those cases where a certain attribute or attributes are used with a given saint in Mexico and New Mexico, and these are not used in European art, a careful examination of the life of the saint will show the appropriateness of them. A case in point is the stand-up collar, chain and medallion worn by St. Cajetan in Mexican and New Mexican representations.

There is nothing indigenous about either the saints or their symbols and attributes found in New Mexican folk art, so an extensive knowledge of Christian iconography and hagiography is absolutely indispensable to a proper study of New Mexican *santos.*

---

1. Roberto Montenegro, *Retablos de Mexico, Mexican Votive Paintings,* Mexico, 1950.

APPENDIX B

REPRESENTATIONS IN NEW MEXICAN RELIGIOUS FOLK ART[1]

1. REPRESENTATIONS OF CHRIST

Aside from the many forms of the Sacred Monogram IHS (which rarely appears in New Mexican folk art) and the hundreds of forms of the Cross, there are 79 symbols of Christ, 26 of which are found in *santero* simulacra. To these 26 symbols of Christ we can add 13 different crosses out of the 50 that have been used in Christian symbolism, and 17 symbols of Our Lord's Passion out of the recognized 35. Thus, out of a total of 164 symbols of Christ, 56 appear in the works of the New Mexican folk image-maker with the following 19 different representations:

1. *La Santísima Trinidad,* The Most Holy Trinity. 2. *La Huida a Egipto,* The Flight into Egypt. 3. *El Santo Niño,* The Christ Child. 4. *La Sagrada Familia,* The Holy Family. 5. *El Divino Pastor,* The Divine Shepherd. 6. *El Niño Perdido,* The Lost Christ Child. 7. *El Santo Niño de Atocha.* The Christ Child of Atocha. 8. *Jesús Nazareno,* The Man of Sorrows. 9. *La Coronación de Espinas,* The Crowning with Thorns. 10. *La Flagelación de Jesús,* The Scourging at the Pillar. 11. *Jesús es Cargado con la Cruz,* Jesus Carries His Cross. 12. *El Divino Rostro,* Veronica's Veil. 13. *Cristo Crucificado,* Christ Crucified. 14. *El Santo Entierro,* Christ in the Sepulcher. 15. *El Sagrado Corazón de Jesús,* The Sacred Heart of Jesus. 16. *La Fuente de la Vida,* The Font of Life. 17. *Alegoría de la Redención,* Allegory of the Redemption. 18. *Nuestro Señor de Esquípulas,* The Christ of Esquípulas. 19. *La Vara de Jesé,* The Rod of Jesse.

2. REPRESENTATIONS OF THE VIRGIN

As Christian art developed, it became increasingly necessary to employ more and more symbols and attributes for the clarification of specific ideas relating to the Virgin and for the representation of the hundreds of special advocations of her. Of the 20 principal symbols and attributes of Mary, all appear in New Mexican folk art. The colors of the Virgin are traditionally: Red, love; White, purity; and Blue, truth. The New Mexican *santeros* did not pay too much attention to traditional colors. In the case of Marian representations, almost any combination of shades of green, yellow, red, brown, and blue may be found applied to the robe, dress, cape, hood, mantle, lining of mantle, skirt, or veil. Of the myriad titles evolved for the Virgin out of history, legend, or the needs of suffering humanity, 19 are found in New Mexican folk art:

1. *N. S.*[2] *de la Inmaculada Concepción,* Our Lady of the Immaculate Conception. 2. *N. S. de la Anunciación,* Our Lady of the Annunciation. 3. *N. S. de la Candelaria,* Our Lady of the Purification. 4. *María al Pie de la Cruz,* in the same situation as 5. *N. S. de los Dolores,* Our Lady of Sorrows, and depicted in the same way in New Mexico. 6. *Pietá.* 7. *N. S. de la Soledad,* Our Lady of Solitude. 8. *N. S. del Carmen,* Our Lady of Mt. Carmel. 9. *N. S. de Guadalupe,* Our Lady of Guadalupe. 10. *N. S. del Patrocinio.* Our Lady of Protection. 11. *N. S. Refugio de Pecadores,* Our Lady Refuge of Sinners. 12. *N. S. del Socorro,* Our Lady of Help. 13. *N. S. del Rosario,* Our Lady of the Rosary. 14. *N. S. de la Manga,* Our Lady of the Cape. 15. *N. S. del Camino,* Our Lady of the Way. 16. *N. S. la Reina* (or *Soberana*) *de los Cielos,* Our Lady Queen of Heaven. 17. *N. S. de la Luz,* Our Lady of Light. 18. *N. S. de los Ángeles,* Our Lady Queen of Angels. 19. *N. S. de Talpa,* Our Lady of Talpa.

1. As representations of Christ and the Virgin only in the rarest of cases present problems of identification, no symbols or attributes will be listed for them.
2. N. S.—*Nuestra Señora,* Our Lady.

3. REPRESENTATIONS OF THE SAINTS WITH THE PRINCIPAL INVOCATIONS AND PATRONAGE IN NEW MEXICO

Sixty-three saints and holy persons have been identified in New Mexican folk art:

1. The Guardian Angel: Patron of children. Against the temptations of the devil. 2. Michael the Archangel. 3. Raphael the Archangel. 4. Gabriel the Archangel. 5. The Boy Tobias. 6. The Prophet Moses. 7. The Prophet Elias. 8. Melchisedech. 9. John the Baptist: Patron of sheepmen and shepherds. 10. Joachim. 11. Ann. 12. Joseph, Conf.: Patron of fathers. For a happy death. 13. Mary Magdalen. 14. Veronica, Martyr. 15. Dismas, the Good Thief. 16. Longinus, Martyr. 17. Peter, Apostle and Martyr: For a happy death. 18. James the Greater, Apostle and Martyr: Patron of soldiers, citizens on a military mission, horses. For the fertility of mares. 19. Matthew, Apostle, Evangelist and Martyr. 20. John, Apostle and Evangelist. 21. Bartholomew, Apostle and Martyr: Against lightning and a fearful death. By women in childbirth. 22. Processus, Martyr. 23. Martinian, Martyr. 24. Acacius of Mt. Ararat, Martyr. 25. Apollonia of Alexandria, Virgin and Martyr. 26. Christopher of Lydia, Martyr. 27. Lawrence, Deacon and Martyr. 28. Athenogenes, Bishop and Martyr. 29. Liberata, Virgin and Martyr. 30. Lucy, Virgin and Martyr. 31. Barbara, Virgin and Martyr: Against lightning. 32. Jerome, Priest and Doctor: Against lightning. 33. Martin of Tours, Bishop and Conf. 34. Augustine of Hippo, Bishop, Conf. and Doctor. 35. Patrick, Bishop and Conf. 36. Giles of Languedoc, Abbot and Conf. 37. Bernard of Clairvaux, Abbot and Doctor. 38. Isidore the Husbandman, Conf.: Patron of agriculture. For all work and against all troubles of the farmer and farm laborer. Carried through fields with Our Lady of Guadalupe. 39. Rosalia of Palermo, Virgin and Hermitess: At wakes, for the deceased. 40. Dominic of Guzman, Conf. 41. Francis of Assisi, Conf.: Patron of Santa Fe. For everything. 42. Hyacinth, Conf. 43. Clare of Assisi, Virgin. 44. Anthony of Padua, Conf.: Finder of lost articles. Patron of home. By young women for worthy husband. By married women for fertility. Animals blessed on his feast, June 13. 45. Ferdinand, King and Conf. 46. Raymond Nonnatus, Conf.: Patron of midwives. By expectant mothers. 47. Bonaventure, Conf. and Doctor. 48. Thomas Aquinas, Conf. and Doctor. 49. Margaret of Cortona, Penitent. 50. Gertrude the Great, Virgin and Abbess. 51. Elizabeth of Portugal, Queen and Widow. 52. Roch, Conf.: Against plagues, infectious diseases. Confused in New Mexico with Lazarus the Beggar. 53. John Nepomucene, Priest and Martyr: Patron of irrigation. 54. Vincent Ferrer, Bishop and Conf. 55. Blessed Lydwina of Schiedam. 56. Rita of Cascia, Widow: Advocate of the impossible. 57. Cajetan, Conf. 58. Francis Xavier, Conf. 59. Ignatius Loyola, Conf. 60. Teresa of Avila, Virgin, Mystic and Doctor. The only woman doctor of the Church. 61. Philip Neri, Conf. 62. Philip of Jesus, Martyr. 63. Turibius of Mongrobejo, Bishop and Conf.

Inez, invoked for the recovery of strayed livestock, and Aloysius Gonzaga, invoked by women in childbirth, have so far not been found in *santero* art.

No commentary on the saints in New Mexican life would be complete without a few words about the popularity of three inventions of well-meaning romancers during the early years of Christianity: Acacius, Liberata and Barbara.

St. Acacius of Mt. Ararat was a supposed martyr of the middle of the second century, whose feast is June 21 in some places and June 22 in others. There are nineteen Acacius and one Acacia listed in Holweck, all considered saints in some part of Christendom. Thirteen of these were martyrs, six by decapitation, with no record of how six others met their fate. The remaining Acacius of Mt. Ararat is the only one who supposedly died by crucifixion. His story was unknown before 1371, when it appeared in the martyrology of Peter de Natalibus. According to the best authorities, the narrative of Acacius is a complete fabrication of the fourteenth century.

He is not mentioned in Thurston's edition of Butler nor in any modern calendar. In Spain this fiction was carried so far as to make Spaniards of Acacius and his companions, and in some Spanish breviaries the lections for the feast are taken from the apocryphal acts. Supposed relics of Acacius and his ten thousand companions are distributed over Western Europe. Up to this day the story of Acacius is unknown to the entire Orient, including Armenia where he was supposed to have died. His history relates how, in consequence of the apparition of an angel, he and nine thousand Roman soldiers were converted during a campaign against certain Syrian tribes, after which they retired to Mt. Ararat in Armenia for a contemplative life. The Emperor Hadrian (A.D. 76–138), and later Antoninus Pius (A.D. 138–161) tried in vain to return them to military service. Instead, the one thousand legionnaries sent to subdue them were converted, and after a series of absurd miracles and long torture they were all either thrown over the cliffs of Mt. Ararat, beheaded, or crucified. The second quake following their crucifixion caused them to be released from their crosses, whereupon they were caught by angels and buried.

Acacius is not always shown crucified in European art. Spanish missals point out that his chief attribute is a crown of thorns, although not one representation of him has been found in Spain by the author. Neither is he found in any of the many lives of the saints printed in Spanish consulted. In Germanic art, where he is most often represented, only Dürer crowns him with thorns. Not one of the twenty images listed by Künstle[2] shows him with this attribute.

St. Acacius was thrice honored in the geographic history of New Mexico. Today there are a dam and a village which bear his name. Two churches are named after him, at Cañon Largo and Las Golondrinas. The village of San Acacio, strangely enough, does not have a single image of its patron. There is also a San Acacio in southern Colorado.

New Mexican representations of St. Acacius are most common, both in *bulto* and *retablo* form, and are, more often than not, the most naïve of all *santero* simulacra. Only two *bultos* of him are known to the author that are not of the Mora Group. He is always shown nailed to a cross, generally crowned with thorns, and fully dressed, usually in the attire of a gentleman of the eighteenth or nineteenth century. A number of soldiers are generally in attendance, sometimes four or six in the case of *bultos,* sometimes a veritable army in the case of *retablos*. A bandoleer over one shoulder and across the breast, and a drum or two at the foot of the cross or somewhere in the picture, are other frequent New Mexican attributes.

Another purely mythical saint rather frequently portrayed in New Mexican folk art is Liberata, a supposed virgin and martyr of the third century. Her feast is July 20. Known as Librada in Spanish-speaking countries, Livrade in France, Uncumber in England, Ontkommer, Kümmernis and Wilgefortis in Germany, her story is a conglomeration of as many fantastic legends as there are similar yarns of martyrdom, and "has the unenviable distinction of being the most obviously false and preposterous of the pseudo-pious romances by which simple Christians have been deceived or regaled." (Thurston, *Butler's Lives of the Saints*). She was one of nine sisters delivered at one birth, which minor detail of her biography will give an idea of the egregious character of her narrative.

St. Liberata has been particularly venerated in Sigüenza, Spain, since about 1300, and is still well known throughout that country. Her body purportedly rests under the altar in the Capilla de Santa Librada, Cathedral of Sigüenza. As in the case of Acacius, Giles, Procopius and a few other saints, Liberata is little-known in Mexico, although there are minor traces of a *cultus* there. Small *bultos* of her exist in Mexico, dating from around the first part of the nineteenth century, and her popularity in New Mexico must have found its origin in the former viceroyalty about that time.

---

2. *Ikonographie der Christlichen Kunst,* II.

Liberata is always represented in European art as a beautiful maiden. Outside of Spain she is always shown nailed to a cross and bearded.[3] In Spanish art there is a single and exceptional instance of her depicted with a beard, and in New Mexican folk art she is never thus represented. She is not too commonly presented in *bultos*, but is quite common on *retablos*.

Good old St. Barbara, presumed to have been a virgin and martyr of the third or fourth century, is yet another bizarre saint who was sneaked into the calendar during the early centuries of Christianity. It is not known where or when she suffered martyrdom, her legend is now considered spurious, and there is grave doubt that she ever existed.

It was from the town of Santa Barbara, some two hundred eighty miles south of El Paso, that Oñate set out for the conquest and colonization of New Mexico on January 26, 1598. She was thrice honored in the geographic history of New Mexico, but today only a land grant and a river bear her name. She is frequently portrayed in *santero* art, where she may be easily identified by her crown and tower, which are her special attribute and symbol in all art. When not crowned, she holds the palm of martyrdom, but may be shown with both of these symbols.

During the age of martyrs, that is, from the time of the crucifixion of St. Peter in A.D. 66 or 68 to the Edict of Milan in 313, Christians died by the thousands throughout the Roman Empire. Although the Church was small (perhaps less than ten per cent of the population) it wielded considerable power. The percentage of literates in those days was less than negligible. The stories of martyrdom transmitted by word of mouth from person to person and from generation to generation, attained ridiculous but very explainable proportions. It would be trying to exaggerate the reaction of the surviving Christians to the Edict of Milan. Almost overnight, the tempest of persecution was followed by a scarcely understandable calm, cruel oppression was followed by complete religious liberty, and from suffering the multiple sorrows of the hunted, Christians suddenly enjoyed the harvest of victory. These factors explain the enthusiasm, the elation, the sensation of utter relief of Christians who were now free to relate in hyperbolical details the sufferings and deaths, and therefore triumphs of brother, sister, father, mother, or friend. It is thus very easy to see how the simple, pious people of colonial New Mexico should have been attracted to the fanciful and melodramatic legends of Acacius, Liberata and Barbara. However, for these three imagined saints, there are sixty whose lives are sufficiently documented to be accepted by the most learned, and who still enjoy their well-earned popularity in New Mexico.

It is interesting to note in connection with the fantastic legends of many early saints that the Spanish liturgist Francisco de Quiñones, a Franciscan, was the first to suppress purely fictional saints in his famous *Breviarium Sanctae Crucis* of 1535. Although his reformed Breviary met with public disapproval, and with the condemnation of the liturgists and theologians of the Sorbonne, it eventually formed the basis of the unfinished Breviary of the Council of Trent and of the *Breviarium Pianum* of Pius V in 1568. Quiñones' insistence on the suppression of fictional saints is reflected in the modern Breviary compiled under Pius IX and Leo XIII.[4]

---

3. The history of bearded women throughout the ages contains enough materials for volumes. Cults arose and departed through the years, some of them, particularly in the Near East, of a revolting character. For an introduction to the subject see Schürer and Ritz, *Sankt Kümmernis und Volto Santo*, Düsseldorf, 1934.

4. *See* Jules Baudot, *Le Breviaire Romain*, Paris, 1907, pp. 89–122.

APPENDIX C

DISTRIBUTION OF IMAGES IN
"INVENTORIES OF CHURCH FURNISHINGS
IN SOME OF THE
NEW MEXICO MISSIONS 1672"[1]

Church	*Statues*	*Paintings on Canvas*	*Paintings on Copper*	*Paintings on Wood*
San Miguel de Taxique	7	"many"	"many"	"painted retablos"
La Natividad de Chililí		4		
N. S. de Socorro	3	3	1	
San Esteban de Ácoma	3 "images in the round"	"paintings" "more canvases"		
N. S. de la Limpia e Inmaculada Concepción de Halona	"images"			
N. S. de la Candelaria de Hawikuh	1	"many canvases"		
San Miguel de Oraibi	"many images in the round" 2	"many paintings" 1		
Xonogopaui	"many images in the round" 1	"many . . . paintings" 1		

---

1. Taken from the article with this title by France V. Scholes and Eleanor B. Adams, *Dargan Historical Essays,* University of New Mexico Publications in History No. 4.

APPENDIX D

DISTRIBUTION OF SACRED IMAGES
LISTED IN THE DOMÍNGUEZ REPORT OF 1776

1. Images in the round	*5. Oil, base material unidentified*	*9. Prints*
2. Crucifixes	*6. Oil on copper*	*10. Colored prints*
3. Bas-reliefs	*7. Oil on buffalo skin*	*11. Unidentified*
4. Oil on canvas	*8. Tempera on buffalo skin*	*12. Totals*

Church	1	2	3	4	5	6	7	8	9	10	11	12
San Francisco, Santa Fe	17	6		45				20[1]		6	1	95
N. S. de la Luz, Santa Fe	3	1	6	17							1	28
San Miguel, Santa Fe	1			8								9
San Diego de Tesuque				1				7				8
San Francisco de Nambé	1	3		2				1	1			8
N. S. de Guadalupe de Pojoaque				5					15			20
San Ildefonso	2			5	3	6		9	1	12		38
Santa Cruz de la Cañada	10	1		2			4	4				21
San Juan	4							2				6
Chapel, N. S. de la Soledad, Rio Arriba	1											1
San Lorenzo de Picurís	1			2				4				7
San José de Trampas	1											1
San Jerónimo de Taos	5			1				18				24
Santa Clara	6			5				3				14
Santa Rosa de Abiquiú	1			1		1		5	16			24
Santo Domingo	4	1		14	2			2				23
San Francisco de Sandía	2			6					6			14
San Felipe de Neri de Albuquerque	8			13					2			23
Chapel, N. S. de la Inmaculada Concepción, Alameda	2			6								8
N. S. de la Inmaculada Concepción, Tomé	2			14								16
San Buenaventura de Cochití				4					4			8
San Felipe	3			6								9
Santa Ana	1			6					4			11
N. S. de la Asunción de Zía	2			4				4				10
San Diego de Jémez	1			2				3				6
San José de Laguna	1	1		1			4	2				9
San Esteban de Ácoma	1			2				1	5[2]			9
N. S. de Guadalupe de Zuñi	3		1	3				3				10
San Agustín de Isleta	5	1		1			5	4				16
N. S. de los Ángeles de Pecos				20				7				27
N. S. de los Remedios de Galisteo				1								1
TOTALS	88	14	7	197	5	7	13	99	54	18	2	504

1. "Some in oils."

2. Three of these are arbitrarily counted, for the inventory states "some little paper prints."

APPENDIX E

DISTRIBUTION OF IMAGES IN THE ROUND (R) OIL PAINTINGS (O) AND PAINTINGS ON WOOD (W) IN THREE CHURCH INVENTORIES

Church	1776[1]			1796[2]			1806[3]		
	R	O	W	R	O	W	R	O	W
San Francisco	17	45	0	9[4]	55[4]	0[5]	No inventory		
Castrense	3	17	0	1	2	0	"	"	
San Miguel Chapel	1	8	0	No inventory			"	"	
Tesuque	0	1	0	"	"		"	"	
Nambé	1	2	0	0	1	0	Images not listed		
Pojoaque	0	5	0	No inventory			1[4]	0	0
San Ildefonso	2	5	0	"	"		No inventory		
Santa Cruz	10	2	0	18	23	0[4]	"	"	
San Juan	4	0	0	2	0	0	"	"	
Picurís	1	2	0	No inventory			"	"	
Trampas	1	0	0	"	"		"	"	
Taos	5	1	0	4	2	3	"	"	
Santa Clara	6	5	0	No inventory			Images not listed		
Abiquiú	1	1	0	2	0	0	"	"	"
Santo Domingo	4	14	0	No inventory			5	8	0
Sandía	2	6	0	2	1	1	No inventory		
Albuquerque	8	13	0	9	8	0	"	"	
Tomé	2	14	0	No inventory			"	"	
Cochití	0	4	0	0	3	0	"	"	
San Felipe	3	6	0	4	4	0	"	"	
Santa Ana	1	6	0	2	5	0	No inventory		
Zía	2	4	0	4	11	0	4	17	4
Jémez	1	2	0	No inventory			1	2	1
Laguna	1	1	0	"	"		No inventory		
Ácoma	1	2	0	3	9	0	"	"	
Zuñi	3	3	0	No inventory			"	"	
Isleta	5	1	0	10	2	0	"	"	
Pecos	0	20	0	No inventory			"	"	
Galisteo	0	1	0	"	"		"	"	
TOTALS	85	191	0	70	126	4	11	27	5
TOTALS FOR YEARS		276			200			43	

1. Domínguez, *op. cit., passim.*
2. *S.A.M.N.M.*, Archive 1360.
3. *Ibid.*, Archive 1993.
4. Plus "others," as stated in the record.
5. Includes the images belonging to the Confraternity of Our Lady of the Rosary, a parish organization.

APPENDIX F

PAINTINGS ON ANIMAL SKIN
LISTED IN THREE CHURCH INVENTORIES

Church	*1776*[1]	*1796*[2]	*1806*[3]	*1959*
San Francisco, Santa Fe	20	4	0	0
Tesuque	8	0	0	0
Nambé	0	0	0	0
San Ildefonso	9	0	0	0
Santa Cruz	8	7	0	0
San Juan	2	0	0	0
Picurís	4	0	0	0
Taos	18	0	0	0
Santa Clara	3	0	0	0
Abiquiú	5	0	0	0
Santo Domingo	2	0	0	1
Zía	4	5	2	0
Jémez	3	0	1	0
Laguna	6	0	0	1
Ácoma	1	0	0	0
Zuñi	3	0	0	0
Isleta	16	0	0	0
Galisteo	0	0	0	2
TOTALS	112	16	3	4

1. Domínguez, *The Missions of New Mexico, 1776, passim.*
2. *S.A.M.N.M.*, Archive No. 1360.
3. *Ibid.*, Archive No. 1993.

APPENDIX G

EXISTING PAINTINGS ON ANIMAL SKINS[1]

1. Inscribed: *Ymagen Milagrosa de Nuestra Señora de Begoña. 1608.*[2] Church of N. S. de los Remedios, Galisteo. Elkskin. 42″ × 56″.

2. *N. S. de Guadalupe.* Once in the Museum of New Mexico. Stolen in 1946.

3. *N. S. de Guadalupe.* Charles D. Carroll Collection. 19¾″ × 29½″.

4. *Santiago.* New Mexico Historical Society. Museum of New Mexico. Elkskin. 33″ × 33″.

5. *Santiago.* Church of Santo Domingo, Santo Domingo Pueblo. Buffalo skin. 35″ × 44″.

6. *Christ Washing the Feet of the Disciples.* Museum of New Mexico. Very faded. Made of two buffalo skins. Most elaborate and ambitious of all skin paintings. 40″ × 100″.

7. *The Crucifixion.* New Mexico Historical Society. Museum of New Mexico. 27″ × 35½″.

8. *The Crucifixion.* Church of N. S. de los Remedios, Galisteo. Elkskin. 42″ × 56″.

9. *The Crucifixion.* New Mexico Historical Society. Museum of New Mexico. 52½″ × 62″.

10. *The Crucifixion.* New Mexico Historical Society. Museum of New Mexico. Dilapidated condition. 29″ × 41″.

11. *The Crucifixion.* Property of Mr. F. H. Douglas, Denver, Colo. Similar to Nos. 7 and 9. 54¾″ × 47½″.

12. *The Creation.* Museum of New Mexico. Mutilated condition. Lower part deliberately cut out very irregularly. Remaining portion measures 35½″ × 48½″.

13. *St. Joseph and the Christ Child.* Church of San José de Laguna. Elkskin. Very fine condition, although lower third is water stained. 56″ × 68″.

14. *St. John the Baptist.* Museum of New Mexico. Deerskin. 34″ × 43″.

15. *St. Francis of Assisi.* Property of Mr. Julias Gans, Santa Fe. Buffalo hide. 40″ × 68″. Now hanging in Mr. Gans' curio store on the Santa Fe plaza.

Retouched in heavy, black outlines. Red dots added to habit detract from original conception.

16. *St. Cajetan.* Kleijkamp and Monroe Collection. Deerskin. 26″ × 34½″.

17. *St. Didacus of Alcalá?* Museum of New Mexico. Elkskin. 40″ × 22″.

18. *St. Barbara.* Museum of New Mexico. Deerskin. 38″ × 49″.

19. *The Crucifixion.* The Cathedral Museum, Santa Fe. Deerskin. 44½″ × 67½″.

20. *St. John the Baptist.* The Cathedral Museum, Santa Fe. 32½″ × 44″.

21. *N. S. de Guadalupe.* Mission, Carmel, Calif.

22. *Our Lady.* Fragment. Charles D. Carroll Collection.

23. *St. Anthony of Padua.* Kleijkamp and Monroe Collection. Fragment. 19½″ × 16″.

24. *N. S. de Guadalupe.* Formerly in Seligman Collection. Present whereabouts unknown.

25. *St. Dominic. St. Thomas Aquinas. St. Albertus Magnus.* Museum of New Mexico. Deerskin. 35″ × 58″. Poor condition. Patched.

26. There is in the Museum of New Mexico a painted deerskin measuring 33″ × 33″. Heretofore classified as a folk work, with the possibility of Indian origin, it has been identified as a representation of *Santiago.* In the center is the indistinct figure of a man holding a foreshortened banner in his right hand. The left hand and arm are not visible. He wears a headgear that looks like a three-horned biretta. The figure appears to be astride a horse, but close examination shows that the animal is a later addition. This is the work of an early semilearned painter, scrambled later by more than one hand.

---

1. Skin paintings could have been executed as early as 1600 and as late as 1776.

2. This is only a remote imitation of the famous statue of the same title, patroness of the Basque Provinces and of Bilbao. A photographic reproduction of the Basque statue may be seen in Juan Subías Galter, *Imágenes Españolas de la Virgen*, Lámina XX. Nos. 1, 6, 7, 12, 13, 14 and 16 are similar enough in drawing and colors to say that they were done by the same artist.

APPENDIX H

A SELECTED LIST OF SANTO COLLECTIONS

ARRANGED ACCORDING TO THE DATE OF THEIR INCEPTION

1900 (or before) New Mexico Historical Society, Museum of New Mexico. Collections such as those of Florence McCormick and Norma Fiske Day are regularly being presented to the Museum of New Mexico.

1910 Herbert I. Spinden. Partially housed in The Brooklyn Museum, Brooklyn, but now for sale.

1912 The Fred Harvey Company, Santa Fe and Albuquerque.

1920 Mary C. Wheelwright, Alcalde, New Mexico.

1920 The Harwood Foundation, Taos. Started with the gift collection of Mrs. Mabel Dodge Luhan.

1921 A. Gilberto Espinosa, Albuquerque.

1922 John Gaw Meem, Santa Fe.

1922 Ralph Meyers, Taos. In process of sale since the death of Mr. Meyers.

1927 The Cathedral Museum, Santa Fe. Not a collection in the true sense, since it has not been organized or catalogued.

1932 Cady Wells, Santa Fe. Now part of the Museum of New Mexico.

1935 The Alice Bemis Taylor Collection, Colorado Springs Fine Arts Center, Colorado Springs.

1936 The Denver Art Museum, Denver. Comprised principally of the Anne Evans Collection.

1939 The University of New Mexico, Albuquerque. Comprised principally of the Mrs. Neil B. Field Collection.

1950 The Detroit Institute of Arts, Detroit. The gifts of Mrs. Lillian Henkel Haass and Robert H. Tannahill.

1951 Alfred I. Barton, Miami Beach, Florida.

Other collections of long standing are: Mrs. Cornelia G. Thompson, Nambé, New Mexico; Bruce Cooper, Santa Fe; Jan Kleijkamp and Ellis Monroe, New York, N. Y.;[1] Charles D. Carroll, Taos;[2] Stanley Marcus, Dallas, Texas; Mr. and Mrs. Robert McKinney, Nambé; Albert Barnes, Merion, Pa.;[3] Mabel Dodge Luhan, Taos; Santa Barbara Museum, Santa Barbara, Calif.

1. This collection is now the exclusive property of Mr. Monroe, but for historical reasons is referred to as the Kleijkamp and Monroe Collection. It is made up in part of the former collections of H. K. Gilmore, James MacMillan, and Eleanor Bedell, all of Santa Fe.

2. This is one of the finest private collections, but is rapidly being sold.

3. Secured from the old MacMillan and Seligman collections.

BIBLIOGRAPHY

PRINCIPAL ARCHIVES

A.G.I.—Archivo General de Indias, Seville, Spain.

C.R.—Coronado Room, University of New Mexico Library, Albuquerque.

L.C.—Library of Congress, Washington, D.C.

L.M.N.M.—Library of the Museum of New Mexico, Santa Fe.

S.A.D.I.—Spanish Archives of New Mexico, Department of the Interior, General Land and Survey Office, Santa Fe.

S.A.M.N.M.—Spanish Archives of New Mexico, Museum of New Mexico, Santa Fe.

MANUSCRIPT SOURCES

A.G.   Audiencia de Guadalajara, Legajos 139-42. Films and photostats in C.R. and L.C.

1. Legajo 139.
"Testimonio de Todos los autos sobre el Reconocimiento mandado haçer de Una Mina de Azogue en la Sierra azul de las Provincias de la nueva Mexico; y la entrada que hizo Dⁿ Diego de Bargas a la Conquista que Consiguió de la Reducion de los Apostatas de la Villa de Sᵗᵃ Fee y algunos Pueblos de Su Contorno. Año de 1692." Fols. 520.
"Zacatecas. A. S. M. Mayo a 16 de 1693. Dⁿ Diego de Bargas Zapata y Lujan. Informe a Vta Magᵈ sobre la restauracion y conquista de la Nueba Mexico y sus Provincias que ha hecho a su costa . . ." Fols. 22.
"Govierno. Año 1693. 2ᵃˢ noticias. Testimonio del segundo quaderno en que Prosigue la restauración reducion y Conquista del Reyno de la nueva Mexico Sus Provincias de Zuñi y Moqui y Peñol de Acoma. Por dⁿ Diego de Vargas Su

Govᵒʳ y Capⁿ General—y las providencias en esta corte de Mexico dadas Por el exᵐᵒ señor Virrey conde de Galve Con Aquerdo de Junta Genˡ." Fols. 379.

2. Legajo 140.
"Govierno. Año De 1694. Testimonio de Autos Dela Ultima Enttrada y conquiztta qᵘᵉ hiso Don Diego de Vargas Zapatta Lujan Ponce de Leon Govᵒʳ y cappⁿ Genˡ de las Provincias de la Nueva Mexᶜᵒ a ellas y su Villa de Sancta Fee y Providencias Sobre ttodo Por el Exᵐᵒ señor Conde de Galve Virrey Govᵒʳ y Cappⁿ gˡ de esta Nueba España." Fols. 371.
"Govierno. Año de 1695. Testimonio de autos de la Guerra operaciones y Campañas executadas por Don Diego de Vargas Lujan y Zapata Ponze de Leon Goverᵒʳ de la nueva Mexᶜᵒ Sobre la Conquista de aquel Reyno." Fols. 763.

3. Legajo 141.
"Govierno Año de 1697. Testimonio de los tres Pendimientos que Remitió el Governador de la nueva Mexico Dn Diego de Bargas Zapata lujan Ponce de Leon al exmo señor Obispo Virrey Dn Juan Ortega Montañes; con Inzercion de las Juntas Consultas y Decretos y Demas Proveimientos de dho Exmo Sor Dados en este Particular sobre lo q se Expressa . . ." Fols. 511.
"Govierno Año de 1697. 6 Quano. Testimonio de los autos de grra que a fulminado el Gral Don Diego de Vargas Sapata Lujan Ponse de Leon govor y Cappⁿ Gral del Reino de la Nueva Mexico." Fols. 217.
"Gno. Año de 1698. Autos sobre la contradiccion echa por Parte de don Diego de Vargas Sapata y Luján governador y capitan general de la Nueva Mexico a la Presentacion de las

Rs Cédulas en que su Magd hiço mrd de aquel gno al Castellano don Pedro Rodríguez Cubero." Fols. 20.

S.A.M.N.M. Spanish Archives of New Mexico, Museum of New Mexico, Santa Fe. Archives Nos. 1 to and including 3097, catalogued in Twitchell, *The Spanish Archives of New Mexico, II,* listed *infra* under Printed Works. Archives Nos. 1360 and 1993.

S.A.D.I. Spanish Archives of New Mexico, Department of the Interior, General Land and Survey Office, Santa Fe, New Mexico. Archives Nos. 1 to and including 1384, catalogued in Twitchell, *The Spanish Archives of New Mexico I,* listed *infra* under Printed Works. Archives Nos. 13, 48, 49, 88, 94, 101, 123, 124, 144, 154, 193, 197, 198, 344, 351, 359, 393, 406, 452, 454, 458, 513, 530, 552, 559, 600, 604, 611, 626, 661, and 717.

Bourke, John Gregory. "Field Notes, general and personal, of John Gregory Bourke, U.S. Army, Nov. 18, 1872 to June 8, 1896; source material on the West." Photostats in C.R. Vols. 42, 44 and 45.

PRINTED WORKS

1. SPANISH AND MEXICAN BACKGROUNDS

Adams, Eleanor B. "Bishop Tamarón's Visitation to New Mexico, 1760," *New Mexico Historical Review,* XXVIII, 2 (April, 1953), 81-114.

Ballesteros y Beretta, Antonio. *Historia de España y su influencia en la historia universal.* 9 vols. Barcelona, 1918–41.

Bolton, Herbert Eugene, and Thomas Maitland Marshall. *The Colonization of North America, 1492–1783.* New York, 1920.

Bolton, Herbert Eugene, Ed. *Spanish Exploration in the Southwest, 1542–1706.* Original Narratives of Early American History. New York, 1930.

Díaz del Castillo, Bernal. *Verdadera Historia de los Sucesos de la Conquista de la Nueva-España.* Ed., E. de Vedia, Biblioteca de Autores Españoles, XXVI, Madrid, 1853.

Prescott, William H. *History of the Conquest of Mexico.* 3 vols. New York, 1843.

Romero de Terreros, Manuel. *Arte Colonial.* 3 vols. Mexico, 1816–21.

Sierra, Justo, Ed. *México, Su Evolución Social.* 3 vols. Mexico, 1900–02.

2. NEW MEXICAN HISTORY

Abert, Lieut. John W. "Report of . . . his Examination of New Mexico in the Years 1846–'47," pp. 419–548, W. H. Emory, *Notes on a Military Reconnoissance* . . . . Washington, 1848.

Adams, Eleanor B. *See* Domínguez, Fray Francisco Atanasio; Scholes, France V.

Bancroft, Hubert Howe. *History of Arizona and New Mexico, 1530–1880.* San Francisco, 1889.

Barreiro, Antonio. *Ojeada sobre Nuevo-México* . . . Puebla, 1832. Photostatic copy in H. Bailey Carroll and J. Villasana Haggard, *Three New Mexico Chronicles,* 263–318.

Benavides, Alonso de. *Memorial . . . hecho por el padre Fray Alonso de Benauides* . . . Madrid, 1630. Facsimile in Mrs. Edward E. Ayer, Trans., *The Memorial of Fray Alonso de Benavides 1630.* Chicago, 1916.

———. *Fray Alonso de Benavides' Revised Memorial of 1634.* Eds., Frederick W. Hodge, George P. Hammond, and Agapito Rey, Albuquerque, 1945. Coronado Historical Series, IV.

Bloom, Lansing B. "New Mexico under Mexican Administration, 1821–1846," *Old Santa Fe,* I–III, 1913–16.

———. "Bourke on the Southwest," *New Mexico Historical Review,* VIII, 1 (Jan., 1933), 1–30; XI, 3 (July, 1936), 217–82; XIII, 2 (April, 1938), 192–238.

Bolton, Herbert E. "French Intrusions into New Mexico," *The Pacific Ocean in History.* New York, 1917.

———. *The Spanish Borderlands.* . . . New Haven, 1921. Vol. 23, The Chronicles of America.

Carroll, H. Bailey, and J. Villasana Haggard, Trans. and Ed. *Three New Mexico Chronicles,* Albuquerque, 1942. Quivira Society Publications, XI.

Castañeda, Pedro de. "The Narrative of the Expedition of Coronado," in *Spanish Explorers in the Southern United States, 1528–1543.* New York, 1925. Ed., Frederick W. Hodge, Original Narratives of Early American History.

Chávez, Fray Angélico. *Our Lady of the Conquest.* Santa Fe, 1948.

———. "Saints' Names in New Mexican Geography," *El Palacio,* 56, 11 (November, 1949), 323–35.

———. "How Old is San Miguel?," *Ibid.,* 60, 4 (April, 1953), 141–50.

———. "San José de Chama and its Author," *Ibid.,* 154–60.

———. *La Conquistadora. The Autobiography of*

an Ancient Statue. Paterson, N.J., 1954.

———. *See* Domínguez, Fray Francisco Atanasio.

Craig, Rev. Robert M. *Our Mexicans.* The Board of Home Missions of the Presbyterian Church in the U.S.A. New York, 1904.

Davis, W. W. H. *El Gringo or New Mexico and Her People.* New York, 1857.

Defouri, Rev. James H. *Historical Sketch of the Catholic Church in New Mexico.* San Francisco, 1887.

Dickey, Roland F. *New Mexico Village Arts.* Albuquerque, 1949.

Domínguez, Fray Francisco Atanasio. *The Missions of New Mexico, 1776.* Trans. and Annotated by Eleanor B. Adams and Fray Angélico Chávez. Albuquerque, 1956.

Emory, W. H. *Notes on a Military Reconnoissance from Fort Leavenworth, in Missouri, to San Diego, in California.* . . . 13th Cong., 1st Ses., Ex. Doc. No. 41. Washington, D.C., 1848.

Espinosa, J. Manuel. *Crusaders of the Rio Grande.* Chicago, 1942.

———, Trans. *First Expedition of Vargas into New Mexico, 1692.* Albuquerque, 1940. Coronado Historical Series, X.

Espinosa, Gilberto. *See* Villagrá, Gaspar Pérez de.

Fisher, Reginald. *See* Hewett, Edgar L.

Forrest, Earle R. *Missions and Pueblos of the Old Southwest.* Cleveland, 1929.

Gibson, George Rutledge. *Journal of a Soldier under Kearny and Doniphan, 1846–1847.* Ed., Ralph P. Bieber. Glendale, Calif., 1935. Southwest Historical Series, III.

Gregg, Josiah. *Commerce of the Prairies. The Journal of a Santa Fe Trader.* Dallas, Texas [1933]. Orig. ed., 2 vols. New York, 1844.

Hackett, Charles Wilson, Ed. *Historical Documents Relating to New Mexico, Nueva Vizcaya, and Approaches Thereto to 1773.* Collected by Adolph F. A. Bandelier; Spanish text and English trans. 3 vols. Washington, D.C., 1923–37.

———, and Charmion Clair Shelby. *Revolt of the Pueblo Indians of New Mexico and Otermin's Attempted Reconquest 1680–1682.* 2 vols. Albuquerque, 1942. Coronado Historical Series, VIII–IX.

Haggard, J. Villasana. *See* Carroll, H. Bailey.

Hammond, George P. *Don Juan de Oñate and the Founding of New Mexico.* Santa Fe [1927].

———, and Agapito Rey. *Narratives of the Coronado Expedition, 1540–1542.* Albuquerque, 1940. Coronado Historical Series, II.

———. *See* Benavides, Alonso de.

———. *See* Pérez de Luxan, Diego.

Henderson, Alice Corbin. *Brothers of Light. The Penitentes of the Southwest.* New York [1937].

Hewett, Edgar L., and Wayne L. Mauzy. *Landmarks of New Mexico.* 2nd ed. Albuquerque, 1947.

———, and Reginald Fisher. *Mission Monuments of New Mexico.* Albuquerque, 1943.

Hodge, Frederick W. *See* Benavides, Alonso de.

———. *See* Castañeda, Pedro de.

Howlett, Rev. W. J. *Life of the Right Reverend Joseph P. Machebeuf, D. D.* Pueblo, Colo., 1908.

Ingersoll, Ernest. *The Crest of the Continent.* Chicago, 1885.

James, George Wharton. *New Mexico, The Land of the Delight Makers.* Boston [1920].

Johnston, Capt. A. R. "Journal of Captain A. R. Johnston. First Dragoons," pp. 567–614, W. H. Emory, *Notes on a Military Reconnoisance* . . . , Washington, D.C., 1848.

Kendall, George Wilkins. *Narrative of the Texan Santa Fe Expedition, 1841.* New York, 1844.

Kubler, George. "The Religious Architecture of New Mexico in the Colonial Period and Since the American Occupation," *Contributions of the Taylor Museum.* Colorado Springs, Colo., 1940.

Lummis, Charles Fletcher. *The Land of Poco Tiempo.* New York, 1893.

Maas, P. Otto. *Misiones de Nuevo Méjico, Documentos del Archivo General de Indias (Sevilla) publicados por primera vez y anotados.* Madrid, 1929.

———. *Viajes de misioneros Franciscanos a la conquista del Nuevo México.* Sevilla, 1915.

Magoffin, Susan Shelby. *Down the Santa Fe Trail and into Mexico. The Diary of Susan Shelby Magoffin.* New Haven, 1826.

Mauzy, Wayne L. *See* Hewett, Edgar L.

Meline, James F. *Two Thousand Miles on Horseback. Santa Fe and Back.* New York, 1868.

Möllhausen, Baldwin. *Diary of a Journey from the Mississippi to the Coasts of the Pacific* . . ., Trans., Mrs. Percy Sinnett. 2 vols. London, 1858.

Peixotto, Ernest. *Our Hispanic Southwest: Arizona, Texas, and New Mexico.* New York, 1916.

Pike, Zebulon Montgomery. *Exploratory Travels.* Ed., T. Rees. London, 1811.

———. *The Southwestern Expedition of Zebulon M. Pike.* Ed., Milo Milton Quaife. Chicago, 1925.

Pérez de Luxan, Diego. *Expedition into New Mexico Made by Antonio de Espejo, 1582–1583.* Ed. and Trans., George P. Hammond and Agapito Rey. Los Angeles, 1929. Quivira Society Publications, I.

Pino, Pedro Bautista. *Exposición sucinta y sencilla de la provincia del Nuevo Mexico hecha por su diputado en cortes con areglo a sus instrucciones.* Cadiz, 1812.
    Photostatic copy in H. Bailey Carroll and J. Villasana Haggard, *Three New Mexico Chronicles*, 211–61.

Prince, L. Bradford. *Spanish Mission Churches of New Mexico.* Cedar Rapids, Ia., 1915.

Rael, Juan B. *The New Mexican Alabado.* Stanford, Calif., 1951

Rey, Agapito. *See* Benavides, Alonso de.

———. *See* Hammond, George P.

———. *See* Pérez de Luxan, Diego.

Ruxton, George F. *Adventures in Mexico.* London, 1847.

———. *Adventures in Mexico and the Rocky Mountains.* New York, 1848.

Salpointe, Rev. J. B. *Soldiers of the Cross; Notes on the Ecclesiastical History of New Mexico, Arizona, and Colorado.* Banning, Calif., 1898.

Scholes, France V. "The Supply Service of the New Mexico Missions in the Seventeenth Century," *New Mexico Historical Review*, V (1930), 93–115, 186–210, 386–404.

———. "Problems in the Early Ecclesiastical History of New Mexico," *Ibid.*, VII, 1 (Jan., 1932), 132–74.

———. "Civil Government and Society in New Mexico in the Seventeenth Century," *Ibid.*, X, 2 (April, 1935), 71–111.

———. "Church and State in New Mexico, 1610–1650," *Historical Society of New Mexico Publications in History,* VII (June, 1937).

———. "Troublous Times in New Mexico, 1659–1670," *Ibid.*, XI (Jan., 1942).

———, and Eleanor B. Adams. "Inventories of Church Furnishings in Some of the New Mexico Missions 1672," *Dargan Historical Essays*, Albuquerque, 1952, 27–38. University of New Mexico Publications in History, No. 4.

Shelby, Charmion Clair. *See* Hackett, Charles Wilson.

Thomas, Alfred Barnaby. *After Coronado, Spanish Exploration Northeast of New Mexico, 1696–1727.* Norman, Okla., 1935.

———. *The Plains Indians and New Mexico, 1751–1778.* Albuquerque, 1940. Coronado Historical Series, XI.

Twitchell, Ralph Emerson. *The Spanish Archives of New Mexico.* 2 vols. Cedar Rapids, Ia., 1911.

Villagrá, Gaspar Pérez de. *Historia de la Nueva México.* Alcalá, 1610. Trans., Gilberto Espinosa,

History of New Mexico. Los Angeles, 1933. Quivira Society Publications, IV.

Wagner, Henry R. *The Spanish Southwest, 1542–1794. An Annotated Bibliography.* 2 vols. Albuquerque, 1937.

Webb, James Josiah. *Adventures in the Santa Fe Trade, 1844–1847.* Glendale, Calif., 1931.

Whipple, A.W., and J. C. Ives. *Report of Exploration and Surveys for a Railway Route From the Mississippi Valley to the Pacific Ocean.* War Department, Washington, D.C., 1853–54.

Winship, George Parker, Ed. and Trans. *The Coronado Expedition, 1540–1542.* U.S. Bureau of American Ethnology, 14th Annual Report, Part I. Washington, D.C., 1896.

Wislizenus, Dr. *Memoir of a Tour to Northern Mexico . . . in 1846–47.* 30th Cong., 1st Ses.; Misc. Senate Doc. No. 26. Washington, D.C., 1848.

3. MEXICAN COLONIAL SACRED ART IN NEW MEXICO

Adams, Eleanor B. "The Chapel and Cofradía of Our Lady of Light in Santa Fe," *New Mexico Historical Review*, XXII, 4 (Oct., 1947), 327–41.

Boyd, E. "Museum Acquires Painting on Tanned Buffalo Skin," *El Palacio*, 60, 5 (May, 1953), 217–19.

———. "Painting on Wood of Saint Raphael," *El Palacio*, 62, 3 (March, 1955), 67.

Chávez, Fray Angélico. *Our Lady of the Conquest.* Santa Fe, 1948.

———. "Nuestra Señora del Rosario, La Conquistadora," *New Mexico Historical Review*, XXIII, 2 (April, 1948), 94–128; *Ibid.*, XXIII, 3 (July, 1948), 177–216.

———. "Journey's End for a Pilgrim Lady," *El Palacio*, 56, 5 (April, 1949), 99–101.

———. "La Conquistadora is a Paisana," *El Palacio*, 57, 10 (Oct., 1950), 299–307.

———. *La Conquistadora, The Autobiography of an Ancient Statue.* Paterson, N.J., 1954.

Espinosa, J. Manuel. "The Virgin of the Reconquest of New Mexico," *Mid-America*, 7, 2 (1936), 79–87.

Eustis, Edith M. "Eighteenth Century Catholic Stone Carvings in New Mexico," *Liturgical Arts*, I (1932), 112–15.

Kelemen, Pál. "The Significance of the Stone Retable of Cristo Rey," *El Palacio*, 61, 8 (Aug., 1954), 243–72.

Stubbs, Stanley A., and Bruce T. Ellis. *Archaeological Investigations at the Chapel of San Miguel*

and the Site of La Castrense, Santa Fe, New
Mexico. Santa Fe, 1955. Monograph of the School
of American Research No. 20.

Von Wuthenau, A. "The Spanish Military Chapels
in Santa Fe and the Reredos of Our Lady of
Light," *New Mexico Historical Review*, X, 2
(July, 1935), 175–94.

Walker, M. A., *et al. Sacred Paintings on Skin.*
Museum of New Mexico. Santa Fe, 1944.

Unsigned. "An Old Painting: St. Joseph and the
Christ Child," *Albuquerque Tribune*, April 6,
1943. Reprinted in *New Mexico Historical Review*, XVIII, 2 (April, 1943), 191–92.

4. NEW MEXICAN
RELIGIOUS FOLK ART

Barker, Virgil. "Santos and Signs: Likenesses and
Contrasts," *Magazine of Art*, 36, 4 (April, 1943),
129–30.

Beard, Mary R. "American Traditions in the Arts,"
Magazine of Art, 31, 6 (June, 1928), 326–33.

Borhegyi, Stephen F. " The Miraculous Shrines of
Our Lord of Esquípulas in Guatemala and Chimayó, New Mexico," *El Palacio*, 60, 3 (March,
1953), 83–111.

———. "A Retablo by the 'Quill Pen Painter,'"
El Palacio, 64, 7–8 (July, Aug., 1957), 238–42.

———. "The Cult of Our Lord of Esquípulas in
Middle America and New Mexico," *El Palacio*,
61, 12 (Dec., 1954), 387–401.

Bourke, Constance. "Index of American Design,"
Magazine of Art, 30, 4 (April, 1937), 207–11,
260.

Boyd, E. *Saints and Saint Makers of New Mexico.*
Laboratory of Anthropology, Santa Fe, 1946.

———. "New Mexico Santos," *American Antiques
Journal*, IV (April, 1949), 6–9.

———. "A New Mexican Retablo and its Mexican
Prototype," *El Palacio*, 56, 12 (Dec., 1949), 353,
355–57.

———. "The Niño Perdido Painter," *Ibid.*, 57, 1
(Jan., 1950), 11–12.

———. "Nuestra Señora de la Manga," *Ibid.*, 57, 3
(March, 1950), 85–87.

———. "A Tentative Identification," *Ibid.*, 57, 6
(June, 1950), 163, 165.

———. "San Vicente Ferrer, A Rare Santero Subject," *Ibid.*, 57, 7 (July, 1950), 195, 197.

———. "Our Lady of Refuge, From Frascati to
Northern New Mexico," *Ibid.*, 57, 9 (Sept.,
1950), 275, 277.

———. *The Literature of Santos.* Reprinted from
the Spring 1950 issue of *Southwest Review*, University Press in Dallas, Southern Methodist University, 1950.

———. "New Mexican Bultos with Hollow Skirts:
How They Were Made," *El Palacio*, 58, 5 (May,
1951), 145–48.

———. "An Early New Mexican Watercolor,"
Ibid., 58, 6 (June, 1951), 163–64.

———. "Preservation of the Reredos in San Jose
de Laguna Mission, New Mexico," *The Masterkey*, XXV (Jan.–Feb., 1951), 8–13.

———. "The Source of Certain Elements in Santero Paintings of the Crucifixion," *El Palacio*, 58,
8 (Aug., 1951), 235–36.

———. "The Santero Tradition in the San Luis
Valley," *Ibid.*, 58, 7 (July, 1951), 219–20.

———. *Retablos. The Alfred I. Barton Collection.*
Miami Beach, Fla. [1951].

———. "The Herder's Kit," *El Palacio*, 59, 4
(April, 1952), 103.

———. "Santos of the Southwest," *House and Garden* (Dec., 1952), 92, 165.

———. "The Crucifix in Santero Art," *El Palacio*,
60, 3 (March, 1953), 112–15.

———. "Museum Conservation Project at Ranchos
de Taos Mission," *Ibid.*, 60, 12 (Dec., 1953),
414–18.

———. "Spanish Colonial Lenten Exhibition in Art
Gallery," *Ibid.*, 61, 3 (March, 1954), 67–69.

———. "Repair of the Oratorio of San Buenaventura at Chimayo . . ." *Ibid.*, 62, 4 (April, 1955),
99–101.

———. "Santos of San Ysidro Labrador," *El Palacio*, 63, 4 (April, 1956), 99–100.

———."Annual Lenten Exhibit of the Spanish
Colonial Department in the Art Gallery," *Ibid.*,
63, 4 (April, 1956), 116–19.

———. "Señor Santiago de Chimayo," *Ibid.*, 63, 3
(March, 1956), 69–72.

———. "The Only Bulto of Santo Toribio," *Ibid.*,
64 (March, April, 1957), 109–14.

Cahill, Holger. *New Horizons in American Art.*
New York, 1936.

Carroll, Charles D. "Miguel Aragón, A Great
Santero," *El Palacio*, 50, 3 (March, 1934), 49–64.

Cassidy, Ina Sizer. "Santos and Bultos in the Spanish
Archives," *Ibid.*, 59, 2 (Feb., 1952), 51–56.

Chávez, Fray Angélico. "Comments Concerning
'Tomé and Father J.B.R.,'" *New Mexico Historical Review*, XXXI, 1 (Jan., 1956), 68–74.

Cheney, Sheldon, and M. Candler. "Santos—An
Enigma of American Native Art," *Parnassus*, VII
(May, 1935), 22–24.

Cubells, Father José. "History of the Santuario of

Chimayó," "History of the Santuario of Our Lord of Esquípulas of Chimayó," and "History of Our Lord of Esquípulas, Santuario of Chimayó." *Bulletins* of the Church of the Holy Cross, Santa Cruz, New Mexico (mimeographed). [Sept., 1952; Oct., 1952.]

De Huff, Elizabeth Willis. "Desert Saints," *Time*, XLIX, 14 (April 7, 1947), 49.

———. "Santos and Bultos," *Touring Topics*, XXII (Jan., 1930), 50–51, 56.

———. *Say the Bells of Old Missions: Legends of Old New Mexico Churches*. St. Louis, Mo., 1945.

Dickey, Roland F. "Heaven on Earth," Part IV, Chapters 8, 9, and 10, *New Mexico Village Arts*. Albuquerque, 1949.

Ellis, Florence Hawley. "Santeros of Tomé," *New Mexico Quarterly*, XXIV, 3 (Autumn, 1954), 346–53.

———. "Tomé and Father J. B. R.," *New Mexico Historical Review*, XXX, 2 (April, 1955), 89–114; XXX, 3 (July, 1955), 195–220.

Espinosa, Gilberto. "New Mexico Santos," *New Mexico Magazine*, XIII, 3 (March, 1935), 9–11, 43; Part II, XIII, 4 (April, 1935), 22–23, 36–37; Part III, XIII, 5 (May, 1935), 24–25.

———. "New Mexican Santos," *New Mexico Quarterly Review*, VI (Aug., 1936), 181–89. (A summary of the preceding three articles.)

Espinosa, José Edmundo. "Notes on Boyd's Tentative Identification," *El Palacio*, 59, 1 (Jan., 1952), 3–17.

———. "El Arte Popular Religioso de Nuevo México," *Revista Católica*, 77, 23 (Junio 8, 1952), 356–57.

———. "A Little Dutch Girl Far from Home," *El Palacio*, 61, 3 (March, 1954), 70–73.

———. "The Discovery of the Bulto-Maker Ramón Velázquez of Canjilón," *Ibid.*, 61, 6 (June, 1954), 185–90.

Gettens, Rutherford J., and Evan H. Turner. "The Materials and Methods of Some Religious Paintings of Early Nineteenth-Century New Mexico," *Ibid.*, 58, 1 (Jan., 1951), 3–16.

Halseth, Odd S. "Saints of the New World," *International Studio*, XCIV (Sept., 1929), 32–36, 78.

———. Miscellaneous short biographies and descriptions accompanying photographic reproductions of various retablos. *El Palacio*, 25, 12–13, 14–17, 18, 19, 20, 21–22, 23, 24, 25; 26, 2, 3, 4, 5, 6, 9–12, 13–14; 37, 3–4.

Harrington, M. R. "Our Own Santos," *Masterkey*, XIV (July, 1945), 125–26.

Hispanic Society of America. *Santos of New Mexico*. n.d. Monograph.

———. *Ten Panels Probably Executed by the Indians of New Mexico*. 1926. Monograph.

Hood, Margaret Page. "The Stalwart Saints," *New Mexico Magazine* (Aug., 1945), 18–19; 43, 45.

Hougland, Willard. "Santos: New Mexico's Primitive Art," *Southwest Review*, XXXI, 3 (Summer, 1946), 293–98.

———. *Santos. A Primitive American Art*. With an Introduction by Donald Bear. Kleijkamp and Monroe [New York, 1946]. (Contains a catalogue of the Kleijkamp and Monroe Collection.)

Hunter, Russell Vernon. "Santa Ynez of the Penitentes," *Southwest Review*, XXXII, 3 (Summer, 1947), pp. 275–79.

[Lammert, Fr. Agnellus, O.F.M.] "From the Land of Enchantment," *St. Anthony Messenger* (June, 1950), 22–29.

Laughlin, Ruth. *Caballeros*. "Wooden Saints," Chapter XIII. Caldwell, Ida., 1945.

Luhan, Mabel Dodge. "The Santos of New Mexico," *The Arts*, VII (March, 1925), 127–30.

———. "Santos aus Neu Mexiko," *Das Kunstblatt* (Berlin), (Oct., 1927). (Trans. of the above article; different illus.)

MacMillan, James. *Fifteen New Mexican Santos*. Libros Escogidos. Santa Fe, 1941. (Silk screen plates in color, of little value as records.)

Mangravite, Peppino. "Saints and a Death Angel," *Magazine of Art*, XXXIII (March, 1940), 160–65.

Moeddel, Fr. Kevin, O.F.M. "Built with Hands," *St. Anthony Messenger* (Jan., 1951), 29–31.

Mumey, Nolie. "Saints of the Southwest and Their Attributes," *The Brand Book*, Denver, Colorado, IX, 12 (Dec., 1953), 3–[12]. (Does not describe attributes of the saints.)

Pach, Walter. "New Found Values in Ancient America," *Parnassus*, VII (Dec., 1935), 7–10.

Payne, Elizabeth H. "Santos of the Southwest," *Bulletin of the Detroit Institute of Arts*, XXX, 3 and 4 (1950–51), 77–81.

Read, Benjamin M. "El Santuario de Chimayó," *El Palacio*, 3, 4 (Aug., 1916), 81–84.

Sena, José D. "The Chapel of Don Antonio José Ortiz," *New Mexico Historical Review*, XIII, 4 (1938), 347–59.

Spinden, Herbert J. "Santos and Kachinas," *Brooklyn Museum Bulletin* (Feb., 1940).

Sutherland, Mason. "Santos: New Mexico's Primitive Art," in "Adobe New Mexico," *The National*

Geographic Magazine, XCVI, 6 (Dec., 1949), 823.

Tichy, Marjorie F. "The Florence McCormick Collection of Spanish Colonial Art," *El Palacio*, 57, 2 (Feb., 1950), 35–40.

Turner, Evan H. *See* Gettens, Rutherford J.

Wallrich, William L. "The Santero Tradition in the San Luis Valley," *Western Folklore*, X, 2 (April, 1951), 153–61.

Watkins, Francis E. "The Unlucky Santo," *Masterkey*, V (Dec., 1931), 113.

Wilder, Mitchell A., with Edgar Breitenbach. *Santos. The Religious Folk Art of New Mexico.* The Taylor Museum of the Colorado Springs Fine Arts Center, Colorado Springs, 1943.

Wilder, Mitchell A. "New Mexican Santos," Reprinted from *Image* 3: Winter, 1950, for the Taylor Museum of the Colorado Springs Fine Arts Center, Colorado Springs.

———. "Notes on the Exhibition of Santos," *Clearing House for Southwestern Museums News Letter*, No. 61 (June, 1943), 214–16.

———. "New Mexican Santos," *Holiday*, I (Nov., 1946), 58–59.

———. "*Santos. The Religious Folk Art of New Mexico.* [New York], n.d. Monograph, 3 pp. Issued for distribution to visitors to "a special exhibition, opening September 19, 1952, lent by The Taylor Museum . . . to the Metropolitan Museum of Art."

———. *Idem.* The Detroit Institute of Arts [Detroit, Mich.], n.d. Monograph, 3 pp.

Unsigned. "Wooden Saints," *Life*, XXIV (May 3, 1948), 57–58, 60.

Unsigned. "The Madonna in American Art," *Look* (Dec. 19, 1950), 68, 70.

Unsigned. "Two Centuries of Religious Folk Art in New Mexico," *Think*, XVIII, 10 (Oct., 1952), 18–19.

5. CHRISTIAN ICONOGRAPHY AND HAGIOGRAPHY SELECTED

Attwater, Donald. *A Dictionary of Saints.* An Index to the Revised Edition of Alban Butler's *Lives of the Saints.* New York, 1938.

Baring-Gould, Sabine. *Lives of the Saints.* 16 vols. Edinburg, 1914.

Benedictine Monks of St. Augustine's Abbey, Ramsgate, compilers. *The Book of Saints.* New York, 1947.

Bles, Arthur de. *How to Distinguish the Saints in Art.* New York, 1925.

Braun, S.J., Joseph. *Tracht und Attribute der Heiligen in der deutschen Kunst.* Stuttgart, 1943.

Butler, Rev. Alban. *The Lives of the Saints.* Now Edited, Revised, and Copiously Supplemented by Herbert Thurston, S.J., and Donald Attwater. 12 vols. London, 1938.

———. *Lives of the Saints.* Complete Edition, Edited, Revised and Supplemented by Herbert Thurston, S.J., and Donald Attwater. 4 vols. New York [1955–56].

Cook, Walter William Spencer, and José Guidol Ricart. *Pintura e Imaginería Románicas.* Vol. VI of *Ars Hispaniae.* Madrid, 1950.

Drake, Maurice, and Wilfred Drake. *Saints and Their Emblems.* Philadelphia, London, 1916.

Goldsmith, Elizabeth E. *Sacred Symbols in Art.* New York, 1912.

Holweck, Rev. F. G. *A Biographical Dictionary of the Saints.* St. Louis, Mo., London, 1924.

Jaud, M. Abbé L. *Vies Des Saints.* Paris, 1928.

Künstle, Dr. Karl. *Ikonographie der Christlichen Kunst.* 2 vols. Freiburg in Breisgau. Zweiter Band, 1926. Erster Band, 1928.

———. *Ikonographie der Heiligen.* Freiburg in Breisgau, 1926.

Ricci, Elisa. *Mille Santi nel'Arte.* Milan, 1931.

Roig, Juan Ferrando. *Iconografía de los Santos.* Barcelona, 1950.

Sánchez Pérez, José Augusto. *El Culto Mariano en España.* Madrid, 1934.

Schamoni, Wilhelm. *The Face of the Saints.* Trans. by Anne Fremantle. New York [1947].

T. y Rodríguez, Fr. Juan de. *Vidas de los Santos más conocidos y venerados en España y en las Repúblicas Sudamericanas.* 4 vols. Paris, 1908–09.

Trens, Manuel María. *Iconografía de la Virgen en el Arte Española.* Madrid [1947].

Webber, F. R. *Church Symbolism* . . . , Cleveland, 1938.

6. ENCYCLOPEDIAS

The Catholic Encyclopedia. 15 vols. New York, 1913.

Enciclopedia Italiana di Scienze, Lettere ed Arti. 35 vols., Indici. Appendice. Milan, 1929–38.

Enciclopedia Universal Ilustrada. 70 tomos, 10 apéndices. Espasa-Calpe, Barcelona [1907]–35.

index